Controlling the Uncontrollable?

The Great Powers in the Middle East

ROSTRA books

Trondheim Studies in History
Series editor: Professor Per Hernæs

Executive editorial committee:
Professor Tore T. Petersen, NTNU
Professor Ola S. Stugu, NTNU
Professor Steinar Supphellen, NTNU

Contact address:
Professor P. Hernæs
Department of History and Classical Studies
NTNU
N- 7491 Trondheim
Norway
e-mail: perher@hf.ntnu.no

Controlling the Uncontrollable?

The Great Powers in the Middle East

Edited by
Tore T. Petersen

tapir academic press

© Tapir Academic Press, Trondheim 2006
ISBN 82-519-2190-2
ISBN 13 978-82-519-2190-9

This publication may not be reproduced, stored in a retrieval system or transmitted in any form or by any means; electronic, electrostatic, magnetic tape, mechanical, photo-copying, recording or otherwise, without permission.

Grafisk formgivning og tilretteleggelse: PDC Tangen AS
Omslag: Tapir Akademisk Forlag
Printing: Tapir Uttrykk
Binding: Grafisk Produksjonsservice AS
Paper: Gprint 90 g

Tapir Academic Press
7005 Trondheim

Tlf.: 73 59 32 10
Faks: 73 59 32 04
E-post: forlag@tapir.no
www.tapirforlag.no

Contents

Acknowledgements	vi
Foreword	vii
Notes on the Contributors	viii
Introduction TORE T. PETERSEN	x
Pairing off Empires: The United States as Great Britain in the Middle East EDWARD INGRAM	1
Was the Middle East Birth Place the Birth Place of a Common European Foreign Policy? ALAN MILWARD	23
Innocents Abroad? Orientalism and America's New Empire in the Middle East DOUGLAS LITTLE	37
The United States and Israel: The Formative Years PETER L. HAHN	57
Oil, Allies, Anti-Communism, and Nationalism: U.S. Interests in the Middle East since 1945. MARY ANN HEISS	77
Index	97

Acknowledgements

I wish to thank the Faculty of Arts, at the Norwegian University of Science and Technology (NTNU) for generously funding the Anglo-American Middle East conference in Trondheim, May 2–4, 2005 and the subsequent subvention for this book. Nina Sindre and Vera Hamran greatly assisted in bringing the conference about. My greatest appreciation is for the conference participants, flying long distances to take part in the event, and thereafter rewriting their contributions to make this book possible. This is the first book in the Trondheim Studies in History, ROSTRA, and many thanks to the series editor, professor Per Hernæs, for assisting in producing this book.

Tore T. Petersen

Foreword

I am happy to present the first book in a new series, which we have named *ROSTRA BOOKS – Trondheim Studies in History*. This series is the product of a joint effort between Tapir Academic Press and the Department of History and Classical Studies, The Norwegian University of Science and Technology (NTNU), and our aim is to establish a substantial serie, that can contribute to international and national academic debates. We hope that the present and coming books shall attract the attention of the community of professional historians and also gain interest from a wider academic and general public. As series editor, I wish to emphasise that ROSTRA is open to authors of all types of professional historical studies (Social History, Economic History, Political History etc.). Thus, I encourage scholars to submit manuscripts to be considered for publication. All contributions will be duly assessed by the editorial board and by expert readers.

What's in a name? Certainly there is a lot of *history* in ROSTRA, a name borrowed from the famous speaker's platform in the *Forum Romanum*, from which speakers addressed the people, and where many famous speeches in Roman history were delivered. The name originates from the Roman naval victory over Antium in 338 BC. After the battle, six bronze prows, or beaks, from enemy ships were transported to Rome and attached to the front of the speaker's platform as trophies. The Latin for beaks is *rostra*, and the name has since been used for the platform as such.

The ROSTRA label, of course, also carries a symbolic meaning, and adopting the name for our book series signals our ambition to make it a prominent forum for critical debate and continued questioning of so-called «established historical truths» or conventional wisdom. We hope to be able to live up to the challenge embedded in the name, but, to achieve this we depend, first and foremost, on our authors and contributors.

The first Rostra-book, *Controlling the Uncontrollable? The Great Powers in the Middle East*, edited by Tore T. Petersen, certainly offers a critical examination of important world affairs, and conventional interpretations of relations between the actors on the Middle East political scene are contested or rejected. Thus, I believe, the book fulfils our «rostra ideals» thanks to the authors of the various chapters and the editor who are all prominent international scholars. I hereby acknowledge a great debt of gratitude to them all.

Per Hernæs
Series editor

Notes on the Contributors

TORE T. PETERSEN is Professor of International and American Diplomatic History at the Norwegian University of Science and Technology, Trondheim. He is the author of *The Middle East between the Great Powers: Anglo-American Conflict and Cooperation, 1952–7* (Macmillan, 2000) and *The Decline of the Anglo-American Middle East, 1961–1969: A Willing Retreat* (Sussex Academic Press, 2006). His current research interest includes the project *Richard Nixon, Great Britain, the Persian Gulf and the Arabian Peninsula, 1969–1974*.

EDWARD INGRAM is Professor of Imperial History Emeritus at Simon Fraser University and Founder and Editor of *The International History Review*. Born outside Calcutta in the last years of the Indian Empire, he was educated at Balliol College, Oxford, and the London School of Economics and Political Science. Among his most important works are: *The Defence of British India: Great Britain in the Middle East, 1774–1842; The Beginning of the Great Game in Asia, 1828–1834;* and *The British Empire as a World Power*.

ALAN MILWARD taught economic and contemporary history at the University of Edinburgh, the University of East Anglia and the University of Essex, before becoming Professor of Economic History at Stanford University, of European Studies at the University of Manchester Institute of Science and Technology, of Economic History at The London School of Economics and Political Science and at The European University Institute, Florence. He has been visiting professor at the Ecole Pratique des Hautes Etudes, the Universite de Paris 1(La Sorbonne), Munich University, the University of Illinois, Oslo University, Aarhus University, and most enduringly Trondheim University (NTNU), before becoming Senior Reseach Fellow at St.John's College, Oxford.

DOUGLAS LITTLE is Professor of History and Dean of the College at Clark University, where he has taught since receiving his Ph.D. from Cornell University in 1978. His articles have appeared in *Diplomatic History*, the *International Journal of Middle East Studies*, and the *Journal of American History*. His most recent book, *American Orientalism: The United States and the Middle East since 1945* (University of North Carolina Press, 2002), was reissued in paperback in 2004 with a new epilogue on the War in Iraq.

PETER L. HAHN is Professor of history at The Ohio State University and executive director of the Society for Historians of American Foreign Relations. He is the author of *The United States, Great Britain, and Egypt, 1945–1956: Strategy and Diplomacy in the Early Cold War* (The University of North Carolina Press, 1991) and *Caught in the Middle East: U.S. Policy toward the Arab-Israeli Conflict, 1945–1961* (The University of North Carolina Press, 2004).

MARY ANN HEISS (Ph.D., The Ohio State University, 1991), is an Associate Professor of history at Kent State University. Her publications include *Empire and Nationhood: The United States, Great Britain, and Iranian Oil, 1950–1954* (Columbia University Press, 1997), as well as articles in *The International History Review and Diplomatic History* and numerous book chapters. She was named the 2002 recipient of the Society for Historians of American Foreign Relations Stuart L. Bernath Lecture Prize and served for fifteen years on the editorial staff of *Diplomatic History*.

Introduction

In almost every strategy document produced by Anglo-American policymakers in the 1950s and 1960s, a central goal was to prevent Soviet influence, penetration and control of the Middle East, without much elaboration of what the Soviet threat entailed. Steeped in the politics of the cold war, Anglo-American leaders and administrators probably had little need to explain to each other the consequences of increased Communist influence in the Middle East. The irony is, despite much expenditure of treasure and efforts, the Soviets were largely unsuccessful in the Middle East. Even after the Six Day War, when the Soviet Union lavished military assistance on its clients Egypt, Syria and Iraq in an effort to compensate for its failure to prevent the Arab defeat at the hands of Israel, Soviet influence and control in the Middle East was tenuous at best. By 1970, the Soviet Union had acquired air and naval bases in Egypt, and port rights in Syria, Sudan, Iraq and North and South Yemen. But at what costs? As one authority notes: «In return for enabling the Soviets to claim influence, the Arabs expect Moscow to supply loans, weapons, technical advice, diplomatic support, and favorable terms of trade. The obvious question is, Who is exploiting whom in this relationship?».[1] Why, then, the Anglo-American concern about the Soviet Union in the Middle East? The Soviet Union effectively exploited anti-colonial sentiment in East and Southeast Asia, there was a genuine fear that they could successfully duplicate that policy in the Middle East. For the most part, then, the Soviet threat was more potential than real in the Middle East.[2]

The British and American presence and influence have been far more enduring than that of the Soviet Union in the Middle East. Almost ninety years after British soldiers occupied Basra, there are again British troops there. The American involvement in the Middle East has increased steadily since 1945, culminating with the present American war and occupation of Iraq. Britain was the leading Western power in the Middle East between 1945 and 1952. Thereafter Britain was increasingly challenged by Arab nationalism and a growing American presence in the region, leading to a transfer of power from Britain to the United States culminating with the Suez crisis of November 1956. Still, even after Suez, Britain has been a significant presence in the Persian Gulf, even after the British Labour government withdrew from its military bases there in December 1971. British prime minister, Tony Blair,

---

1   Robert O. Freedman, *Soviet Policy toward the Middle East since 1970* (New York: Praeger, 1982), 40–41.
2   John Lewis Gaddis, *We Now Know: Rethinking Cold War History* (Oxford: Claredon Press, 1998), 163–64.

has not joined the 'coalition of the willing' because he has some inherent desire as claimed by his critics to be Bush' poodle. Blair and key members of the government evidently believe that Britain has a major interest in Iraq and the Middle East. Given the long British presence in the area, to this author this is a far more convincing explanation of Blair's policies, than Britain just being dragged into the war because of some wish to please the Americans.

The Norwegian University of Science and Technology thought it therefore highly appropriate to organize a conference on the Anglo-American Middle East in Trondheim May 2 to May 4, 2005. We define the Anglo-American Middle East as British and US areas of common national interest in the region, it may denote both conflict and cooperation, which indeed it has for much of the period after 1945. The term is flexible, changing continuously with differing patterns of Anglo-American interaction in the Middle East. A distinguished group of scholars accepted our invitations and gracefully agreed to rewrite their lectures for inclusion in this book. They also easily transcended the, perhaps, narrow theme of the conference, making their papers a sophisticated discussion, by and large, on how the different great powers have, not always successfully, tried to control the Middle East. Hence the title of this book, *Controlling the Uncontrollable? The Great Powers in the Middle East*.

Edward Ingram compares with a grand sweep the British and the American imperial experience in the Middle East, he notes that too many scholars exaggerates the power of nineteenth-century Great Britain in order to compare it with the present day 'US paramountcy'. While Britain played the great game of empire against Russia for centuries, also in the Middle East, professor Ingram explains that the British as the Americans today put too much reliance on technology: «US smart weapons have proved no more effective in solving political problems in the Middle East than two nineteenth century Western technologies: steam power and automatic weapons». And as Britain learned in Afghanistan in the 1830s, and the Americans are learning in Iraq today; regime change is easier than state building. Alan Milward is on a different tack, explaining how the oil crisis and oil embargo forced the European Common Market to take a new approach towards the Arabs, in the process cutting loose from the American embrace and laying the foundation for a common EU foreign policy. While the Arab-European dialogue has been much maligned lately, it is an important example as Milward shows of European 'soft' power, compared to the American heavy reliance on 'hard' power, and of institution building within the EU.

In his article, Douglas Little deepens our understanding of his concept *American Orientalism* «the tendency to dismiss Muslims as backward, decadent and evil». Muslims do not hate the US as such, but it is American policies of cultural imperialism, economic expansion, and racial hierarchy that fuel the Islamic rage. Little ends his essay with a withering criticism of George W. Bush who has rejected the doctrine of containment in favour of preventive war when invading Iraq, needlessly creating the current imbroglio there. Peter Hahn discusses American-Israeli relations in the period 1945–1961, showing that Israeli and American officials were often at loggerheads on the future of the Jewish state. According to Hahn, a battle for the president's mind raged during the Truman administration between the president's pro-Zionist advisers in the White House and the more pro-Arab State and Defense Departments. Even while the Zionists often won, Truman deeply resented the pressure on him and would turn towards the state department, giving the impression of a vacillating American policy. Eisenhower tried to pursue a more even handed policy, but as Hahn shows, the president could not fully shake the influence of the pro-Israeli lobby. Rounding off the essays is Mary Ann Heiss' account of key episodes of American oil policy sine 1945. Even with the importance of oil, as Heiss explains, the balance of power had by 1974 shifted in favour of the oil producers; that had «shrewdly divided the Atlantic Alliance, pitting the Western Europeans against both the Americans and each other». With this professor Heiss ties in with the starting point of Alan Milward's essay, as well as explaining the major role of the United States in the Middle East after 1974, ending up with the unilateralism of the current American president. But for all the efforts of the United States and other great powers, as these essays so eloquently show, the great powers have, at best, had limited success in controlling the Middle East.

Tore T. Petersen

Trondheim 15 September 2006

Pairing off Empires: The United States as Great Britain in the Middle East

Edward Ingram

Imagine two productions of *Othello* at the Royal Shakespeare Theatre in Stratford upon Avon in the nineteen fifties. One stars the great American singer, Paul Robeson, the other Sir John Gielgud, Britain's finest classical actor. The scene arrives at which Othello must convince the audience of his heroic stature by breaking up a fight among his followers. Robeson, almost shouting the famous line 'Keep up your bright swords, for the dew will rust them', strides into the melée, brandishing his own sword, as if about to throw the other actors into the wings, if not the stalls. The excited audience gasps. Gielgud whispers the line; standing still, sword sheathed, while drawing on a pair of white gauntlets that catch the light. The fight stops; the other actors drift towards Gielgud as if drawn by a magnet. The audience holds its breath. The theatre is silent.

The playing of this scene illustrates the two most common postures of the system leader in a states system: 'waving the big stick' and 'the mailed fist in the velvet glove'. The second is the posture of the hegemon; the first the posture of the empire. Other states, whether allies or rivals, grew accustomed during the cold war to seeing the United States, beyond the western hemisphere, satisfied with the role of hegemon. The occasions on which it waved briefly the big stick, during the Suez crisis of 1956 for one, caused resentment by their rarity: they took onlookers as well as the injured by surprise. Lately, the George W. Bush administration, mistakenly supposing that history has reached its apotheosis in the globalization of early twenty-first century American liberal capitalism, seems to have succumbed to the lure of empire.

American political scientists of the realist turn often fail to distinguish between the hegemon and the empire.[1] The hegemon in an alliance organizes, persuades, and on occasion restrains. The indispensable partner, nonetheless it acts multilaterally, not unilaterally, with the aim of binding others to its cause by accommodation or appeasement. The Bush administration would dislike having that word applied to it. Appeasement smells of Britain and

---

[1] See, e.g., the essays in *America Unrivalled: The Future of the Balance of Power*, ed. G. John Ikenberry (Ithaca and London, 2002).

France in the 1930s; of Neville Chamberlain's supposed failure to stand up to Adolf Hitler. The empire stands firm. It sees itself as outside, or above, the system it manages: it exercises levers to constrain others while unconstrained itself. During the Suez crisis of 1956, Dwight D. Eisenhower taught Sir Anthony Eden the lesson Eden's predecessors in the heyday of the Indian Empire had taught the nizam of Hyderabad and the shah of Iran: that one should be more on guard with one's friends than with one's enemies.[2]

A system leader that waves the big stick must be certain that the stick will not break in its hands: it must not doubt its own military capability. The Powell doctrine, formulated by the former US chairman of the joint chiefs of staff and secretary of state, Colin Powell, assumes that the United States is now able both to choose the occasions on which it will act and to deploy overwhelming force. The events of 9/11 make one wonder. The wearer of the velvet glove relies on prestige rather than capability: on the assumption that other states will not ask whether the mailed fist exists. Its equivalent to the Powell doctrine is gunboat diplomacy, which applies the principle that the more powerful the state, the less force it should need to deploy and the more elegant should be the symbols of its power. The gold embroidery on the ambassador's court dress may conjure more effectively than an infantry division.

The empire as one of two types of leader of a states system must be distinguished from the two other standard types of empire, precisely because both the United States and Great Britain exemplify all three. Both the United States and the United Kingdom resemble the German Empire and the Austrian Empire: states built-up by treaty, purchase, attachment, and conquest, and applying different laws in different parts of the state. Similarly, both the twenty-first century United States and nineteenth-century Great Britain are empires by P. J. Cain and A. J. Hopkins's definition: a world-wide pattern of trade, investment, influence, and leverage rather than territories.[3] Appearances should not mislead. Late nineteenth-century Great Britain, which ruled more overseas territories than the twentieth century United States, had acquired many of them against its will.[4] It had acquired the ones it did want for strategic rather than economic reasons, even if their strategic value lay in trade, raw materials, and investments elsewhere. Although neither of the two annexed territories on the Middle Eastern mainland, one unquestionably succeeded the other as the imperial power in the region.

---

2   For Hyderabad, see Bharati Ray, *Hyderabad and British Paramountcy, 1858–1883* (Delhi, 1988); for Iran, see Edward Ingram *Britain's Persian Connection, 1798–1828: Prelude to the Great Game in Asia* (Oxford, 1992).
3   P. J. Cain and A. G. Hopkins, *British Imperialism: Innovation and Expansion, 1688–1914* (Harlow, 1993), pp. 17–23. One should note that Cain and Hopkins write about British imperialism, not the British Empire.
4   According to Ronald Robinson and John Gallagher, with Alice Denny, *Africa and the Victorians: The Official Mind of Imperialism* (London, 1967). Earlier the British had been more acquisitive. See C. A. Bayly, *Imperial Meridian: The British Empire and the World, 1780–1830* (Harlow, 1989).

The United States has shifted its posture from hegemon to empire partly to reward itself for winning what it sees as a cultural as well as a political victory in the cold war. A comparison of its intervention in Kuwait in 1990–1 with its invasion of Iraq in 2003 illustrates its recent tendency to model its conduct on Britain's conduct in India rather than the Middle East. Britain became the paramount power in nineteenth century India, the empire in the Indian states system, long before Queen Victoria proclaimed herself an empress. But whereas Britain could act as the empire in India, as long as it isolated the Indian states system from the wider world, elsewhere it acted only as the hegemon. The exception was the short period in the 1830s leading to the invasion of Afghanistan in 1839. The ideological assumptions that underpinned the invasion foreshadowed the Bush administration's assumptions in invading Iraq.

Time, by travelling backwards as well as forwards, changes the character of past worlds. When American political scientists and British historians compare the present-day American empire with the nineteenth-century British one, they paint mismatched pictures. In the historian's opinion, the political scientist in search of comparable cases, who travels backwards from what he takes, mistakenly, to be US paramountcy in a unipolar twenty-first century world, exaggerates the power of nineteenth-century Great Britain.[5] The historian, travelling forwards from a nineteenth-century world in which Great Britain made no claim to worldwide paramountcy, wonders whether the twenty-first century United States is seduced by dreams of grandeur.

The Bush administration's favourite words are 'freedom' and 'expects'. Making other people free is said to be the goal of US foreign policy; but the natives are expected not only to accept the offer of freedom but also to show their gratitude. The secretary of state, Condoleeza Rice, spends her time travelling around the world giving freshman civics lectures to presidents and prime ministers, of Belarus on Monday, the Palestinians on Tuesday, Egypt on Wednesday, Iran on Thursday, and Syria on Friday. Her notion of freedom, her expectation of gratitude, and the disappointment the Bush administration feels when others fail to do as it instructs typify the colonialist mentality it inherited from early nineteenth century Great Britain. What Bush and Rice did not borrow from British politicians led by the emblematic Victorian foreign secretary, Viscount Palmerston, who thought that Britain should thwack the less powerful over the head or around the knees once in a while to remind them that Britain had not lost the knack, they owe to British ideologues, among them Jeremy Bentham, James Mill, and Nassau William Senior. They showed their debt most obviously in their actions in Kuwait, Afghanistan, and Iraq.

---

5   Michael W. Doyle, *Empires* (Ithaca, New York, 1986), p. 236; Christopher Layne, 'The Unipolar Illusion: Why New Great Powers Will Rise', *International Security*, xvii (Spring 1993), 5–51.

In a classic account of the partition of Africa, Ronald Robinson and John Gallagher explain how in the eyes of Europeans, under-priveleged nineteenth century Egyptians, by squandering the money they had borrowed, and with it the opportunites for self-improvement offered to them, became delinquent.[6] When the United States annexed the Philippines in 1898, Rudyard Kipling warned it of the probable consequences of taking up the White Man's Burden. The burden lay not in the West's responsibility for improving the lives of others. It resembled Sisiphus' experience with the Stone: others' resentment of the West for trying to lead the them out of their 'loved Egyptian night'. For the Bush administration, others readily become 'Others': everything Americans are not and practitioners of alien cultures seen to be waging culture wars against the United States. That Muslims, or Arabs, are waging such a culture war may be in doubt. There is less doubt that the Bush administration is fighting a Middle Eastern culture war against Islam as Americans conceive of it. Herein lies the attraction for the Bush administration of Great Britain. Palmerston and the governors-general of India in the 1830s, Lieutenant-General Lord William Bentinck and Lord Auckland, were proud of themselves for fighting culture wars in the Middle East and India against both Asiatic absolutism and Hindu and Muslim superstition.

The emptiness of the Middle East suits it to be the ground on which to fight culture wars. Many of the inhabitants nineteenth century Britons and twenty-first century Americans recognize are ghosts, often from a classical or Biblical past, monthly magazine, Hollywood film, or the First World War: Alexander the Great marching through Persia to Afghanistan, Cleopatra seducing Caesar (or Vivien Leigh playing the seduction of Claude Rains), and Lawrence of Arabia blowing up the Hijaz railway disguised as Peter O'Toole.[7] The American scholarly taste for area studies does not necessarily express an interest in the particular areas; Americans, like Britons, measure events in the Middle East against an external standard. L. Carl Brown defines the region as a penetrated system in which the outcomes of events are determined by outsiders who remain unaffected by them.[8] Like Wonderland, which bemuses Alice when size, shape, and time prove unpredictable there, the Middle East for the United States and Britain resembles a pantomime they are directing that entrances its audience with a series of transformation scenes.

The British transformed the Middle East three times. They announced during the Napoleonic Wars that they expected to influence political developments in the region just when their trade with it appeared to go into terminal decline. Levant Company and the East India Company factories were transformed into the Eastern Question and the Great Game in Asia; two attempts to confine the Russian empire to the heartland of central Eurasia and

---

6   Robinson and Gallagher, *Africa and the Victorians*, p. 467.
7   For Americans, see Douglas Little, *American Orientalism: The United States and the Middle East since 1945* (Chapel Hill and London, 2002), ch. 1; Robert D. Kaplan, *The Arabists: The Romance of an American Elite* (New York, 1993).
8   L. Carl Brown, *International Politics and the Middle East: Old Rules, Dangerous Game* (Princeton, 1984), pp. 3–7.

to prevent it from reaching its geopolitical goal of control over the coastal rimlands.[9] The Eastern Question – what should be done to prevent the break-up of the Ottoman Empire – answered itself: the Ottoman Empire could maintain stability in the Middle East without trying to keep order as long as the European states defined it geographically, not politically or culturally. The British saw the Ottoman Empire as an agreed territory with internationally recognized frontiers. Who ruled it, or by what rules, was immaterial.

The Great Game was more difficult to play than the Eastern Question was to answer. In the region between the Ottoman Empire and India the British had to try to devise a crescent of territorial states, some buffers and others clients, agreeable to Russia while nonetheless separating Russia's territories in Central Asia from Britain's territories in India and trade in the Arabian Gulf. Even if cultural historians are right to stress the manner in which maps, like language, became a tool of empire by buttressing Western ideas, the maps were not drawn with that in mind.[10] They offered an alternative to occupation and administration; a means of solving political problems by negotiation in Europe rather than on the ground in Asia, which was likely to prove more expensive as well as more contentious. As long as the great powers were in agreement about the boundaries of the Middle Eastern states, it hardly mattered whether their inhabitants took much notice of them, as half a century of continual fighting between Israelis and Palestinians has proved.

At the end of the First World War the British transformed the Middle East a second time by painting it red on the map. Despite taking over responsibility for stability in the region from the partitioned Ottoman Empire, they took steps to avoid the responsibility for keeping order. The mandates gave them the means of avoiding rather than the opportunity to disguise the imposition of colonial rule.[11] The British presented the Middle East as the copestone of the imperial horseshoe that ran, on the map, from Capetown, through Khartoum, Cairo, and Baghdad to Delhi, Rangoon, Singapore and Sydney. Egypt mattered most, but neither as the route for the Suez Canal, which the British had tried to prevent being built, and which they saw as a greater strategic liability than economic asset, nor as the seedbed of pan-Arab nationalism, which they did their best to ignore. Egypt was the hub of the embryonic web of imperial air routes.

The third transformation scene followed the end of the Second World War. Clement Attlee's Labour government, which aspired briefly to hold on to Britain's world power status despite the partition of the Indian Empire in 1947, dreamed of turning the Middle East into the shield protecting the new, and they hoped profitable, empire to be built in sub-Saharan

---

9   John P. LeDonne, *The Russian Empire and the World, 1700–1917: the Geopolitics of Expansion and Containment* (New York, 1997); idem, *The Grand Strategy of the Russian Empire, 1650–1831* (New York, 2004).
10 Jeremy Black, *Maps and History: Constructing Images of the Past* (New Haven and London, 1997).
11 Elie Kedourie, *England and the Middle East: The Destruction of the Ottoman Empire* (London, 1987, idem, *The Chatham House Version and Other Middle-Eastern Studies* (Hanover and London, 1984), ch. 9.

Africa. Like the Good Fairy with the Wicked Witch, the dream was paired with a nightmare. The Middle East was also to act as the springboard that launched British forces against the Soviet Union in the event of the third world war predicted at the time of the Korean War, if not expected.[12]

The tensions in the 1950s between Great Britain and the United States over the Middle East arose from their different post-war transformations of it. When the United States, in 1947, took over Britain's patronage of Turkey and Greece, it reshaped the Middle East into the Northern Tier.[13] By drawing a geopolitical line through Turkey, Iran, and Pakistan, and turning them into the frontline in the West's containment of Soviet Communism, the United States also took over Britain's role in the Great Game in Asia.[14] And played the game with greater success. The break-up of the Northern Tier in 1979 – when the Pahlavi regime, ousted from Iran, was replaced by an Islamic republic – turned out not to matter. The implosion of the Soviet Union ten years later enabled the United States to draw a new line, further north, across Central Asia. Once Russia's former Central Asian colonies became successor states – Kazakhstan and the others in the group now called the 'Stans' – the West could try to contain Russia within the lines it had itself drawn on the map in the 1860s and 1870s.

Even if the rivalries between Israelis and Palestinians illustrate the potential stability of disorder, and the Suez Canal illustrates the precedence of strategic calculations over economic ones, Middle Eastern oil appears not to be susceptible to transformation. Oil, however, is not merely a post-Second World War phenomenon, but a post cold-war one. The Harry Truman and Dwight Eisenhower administrations measured the significance of every event in the Middle East, even an attack on Western oil supplies, against its likely effect on the cold war.[15] The oil continued to flow even when the Arab states were fighting against Britain or criticizing the United States for its patronage of Israel.

The United States's inheritance from Great Britain's early nineteenth century Middle Eastern culture war is revealed in their common ideology, fondness for technology, and cast of mind. The American radical right (the so-called NeoCons) are heirs to nineteenth century liberalism, not conservatism: Prince Metternich would feel uncomfortable in their company, the Philosophical Radicals and the Political Economists would not. The Bush administration's ideology of freedom, with its stress on democracy, echoes the Earl Grey administration's

---

12   Michael J. Cohen, *Fighting World War Three from the Middle East: Allied Contingency Plans, 1945–1954* (London, 1997); Wm. Roger Louis, *The British Empire in the Middle East, 1945–1951: Arab Nationalism, The United States, and Postwar Imperialism* (Oxford, 1984), chs. 2–3.
13   Bruce R. Kuniholm, *The Origins of the Cold War in the Near East: Great Power Conflict and Diplomacy in Iran. Turkey, and Greece* (Princeton, 1980).
14   Peter John Brobst, *The Future of the Great Game: Sir Olaf Caroe, India's Independence and the Defence of Asia* (Akron, 2005)
15   Mary Ann Heiss, *Empire and Nationhood: The United States, Great Britain, and Iranian Oil, 1950–1954* (New York, 1997)

stress on liberty in preference to equality and community. Neither state, religion, nor tribe in the Middle East shall deny the individual the opportunity for self-improvement expressed in the right to vote.

For the Bush administration, committed to globalization, freedom is manifest in free trade, the watchword of nineteenth century Great Britain. The extent to which the British were willing to lever other states into opening up their territories to trade, by force if necessary, and the extent to which their goods did drive others from the market, are subjects of a long-running dispute.[16] When the British applied leverage in the Middle East, sometimes they did so by invitation or in an attempt to use trade as a strategic weapon to substitute inland for sea power. The Anglo-Ottoman treaty of Balta Liman offers a good example from 1838. In agreeing to lower tariffs on goods imported into the Ottoman Empire, Sultan Mahmud II was trying to undercut the revenues earned by his rival Mehemet Ali from Egyptian and Syrian monopolies.[17] When the Ottomans allowed the British in 1830 to open up a new trade route to Tabriz by way of Trabzon, were not expecting to receive revenues from the trade nor did the British expect much in the way of profits.[18] In the early nineteenth century Middle East, trade routes acted as political symbols as often as commercial vehicles. Strategy was not aimed at the defence of trade and investment: they were promoted as the cheapest method of defence.

The British, who shared the American assumption that values are built into goods, assumed that their factory-made cottons would not only sweep the field clear of Russian and French-made competitors but also promote political revolution in the Middle Eastern states. By the 1830s they were no longer expecting revolution to give them opportunities for annexation, though that had been their assumption at the turn of the eighteenth century during the Marquis Wellesley's regime in India. Americans, who admit their tendency to imperialism, would deny any similar tendency to colonialism. The same might be said of the British imperialism of free trade. Early nineteenth century liberal capitalism worked to a clearly defined order of priorities: trade and investment without rule whenever possible, but with rule when unavoidable. If rule proved inescapable, indirect rule whenever possible, direct rule only when unavoidable.

The Americans inherited Britons' over-confidence in technology. US smart weapons have proved no more effective in solving political problems in the Middle East than the two

---

16 For the classic exchange, which set the terms of debate, see John Gallagher and Ronald Robinson, 'The Imperialism of Free Trade', *Economic History Review*, 2nd series, vi (1953–4), 1–15; D. C. M. Platt, 'The Imperialism of Free Trade: Some Reservations', *Economic History Review*, 2nd series, xxvi (1968), 296–306; idem, 'Further Objections to an "Imperialism of Free Trade", 1830–1860', *Economic History Review*, 2nd series, xxvi (1973), 77–91.
17 Roger Owen, *The Middle East and the World Economy, 1800–1914* (London, 1981), pp. 279–80; John Marlowe, *Perfidious Albion: The Origins of Anglo-French Rivalry in the Levant* (London, 1971), pp. 234–6.
18 Charles Issawi, 'The Tabriz-Trabzon Trade, 1830–1900: Rise and Decline of a Route', *International Journal of Middle East Studies*, i (1971), 18–27.

nineteenth century Western technologies: steam power and automatic weapons. The embryonic machine gun that scattered the troops of Arabi Bey at Tel el-Kebir in 1882 and mowed down the Dervishes at Omdurman in 1898 gave the British control of Egypt and the Sudan. It did not help them to leave as they had wished. Fifty years earlier, in the 1830s, the British were certain that by fitting steam engines to river boats they could extend the range of their sea power far inland; from the Mediterranean to the east coast of the Black Sea, high up the Indus towards Peshawar, and high up the Orontes towards Aleppo and the Tigris towards Mosul. The first would give them a springboard into Transcaucasia, the second a springboard into Afghanistan, and the third and fourth would draw a line across Mesopotamia and Syria that contained Mehemet Ali to the south and proclaimed to Russia, Britain's ability to preserve the territorial integrity of the Ottoman Empire in Asia. Britain's greatest early nineteenth-century soldier, the duke of Wellington, explained the appeal of technology in 1838: 'If this communication by steam ever finds its way into the Indus … a more decisive step will have been taken to establish the influence of England, English commerce and manufactures in Central Asia … than can be taken by any other means.'[19]

The British drew the same conclusion as the Bush administration from their technological prowess: that Queen Victoria's 'Little Wars' would be clean; short, cheap, and with few casualties. Sir Garnet Wolseley, 'our only general' of the late nineteenth century, made his name by orchestrating a series of short campaigns overseas in which he marched into the Red River territory, Ashanti, and Egypt, tempted the enemy into battle, won a nominally decisive victory, and withdrew without dealing with the political consequences before the rains or the hot weather came. His caution derived from the British experience in the First Afghan War, which had shown him the price for entrapment. In fighting such wars, Britain had one advantage over the United States: its army was drawn from outside society. Britain relied for the projection of world-wide military power on the Indian Army, a mercenary force drawn from the Indian states and paid out of the revenues of the Indian Empire.[20] The United States, relying in Afghanistan and Iraq on citizen soldiers, often members of the National Guard, treats every casualty as a fallen hero. And heroes fall only in just wars.

Neill Ferguson may be right to stress that one prerequisite for successful empire-building is missing in the United States. It lacks a service gentry; a highly educated élite willing to make careers overseas in the certainty of promotion, influence, and upward social mobility upon returning home.[21] The Peace Corps will never rival the Indian Civil Service and Paul Wolfowitz was thought to have stepped down by moving from the second most senior post at the defence department to become head of the World Bank. Ferguson, however, underes-

---

19 Memo. by Wellington, 21 November 1838, University of Southampton, Hartley Library, Wellington MSS 2/177/62.
20 Douglas M. Peers, *Between Mars and Mammon: Colonial Armies and the Garrison State in India, 1819–1835* (New York, 1995); David Omissi, *The Sepoy and the Raj: The Indian Army, 1860–1940* (London, 1994).
21 Neill Ferguson, *Colossus: The Rise and Fall of the American Empire* (London, 2004), pp. 204–13.

timates the role of the services in the United States, which is a more militarized empire than nineteenth century Great Britain. The staffs of the five US military commands, whose proconsular commanders-in-chief are no longer subordinate to the joint chiefs of staff, spend much of their careers in short bursts overseas or monitoring overseas developments. No nineteenth century British commander claimed the authority to act with such freedom from metropolitan control as General Douglas MacArthur.

Even if one empire relies on military officers and the other relied on civilian officials, the ethos of both is evident in a shared Utopian cast of mind. The speed at which Donald Rumsfeld expected not merely to topple the Taliban in Afghanistan and Saddam Hussein in Iraq but also to rebuild the political structures of the two states and to change the behaviour of their inhabitants on an American model, without having to provide an alternative administration, is reminiscent of Britain's intervention in Egypt in 1882. William Gladstone's Liberal government assumed that Britain, embodied in Wolseley, could 'rescue and retire' by replacing Arabi Bey's proto-nationalist regime with one willing to accomodate the West by servicing the foreign debt. When the First World War broke out in 1914, the British had yet to work out how to satisfy the competing claims of nationalists and investors.[22]

The early-nineteenth century British élites, who saw Britain as a free society, waged war within the confines of the concert of Europe against the absolutism they associated with the Holy Alliance, just as the United States waged cold war against the Soviet Union at the United Nations.[23] And like the United States, they looked around the wider world and saw tyranny and lack of liberty in all directions. But the liberty they envisaged was of a particular type: liberty as opportunity for individual self-betterment unimpeded by the state. If the state limited its role in society, there would never be the need to reverse its encroachments by privatization, free trade's twin in the quest for globalization. In Bentham's phrase, 'The request which agriculture, manufactures and commerce present to government is as modest and reasonable as that which Diogenes made to Alexander, *Stand out* of my Sunshine'!'[24] Despite Anglo-American individualism's emphasis on the sanctity of private property, the freedom offered by both Britons and Americans takes no account of the need for security, perhaps less surprisingly in Americans, given the level of everyday violence they tolerate in their own lives. The offer of liberty, when tied to a claim to cultural superiority, is bound to lead to a demand for equality. The demand, and the refusal to satisfy it, is bound to lead to disappointment.[25]

---

22 Roger Owen, *Lord Cromer: Victorian Imperialist and Edwardian Proconsul* (New York, 2004).
23 Gunther Heydemann, *Konstitution gegen Revolution: Die Britische Deutschland- und Italienpolitik, 1815–1848* (Gottingen and Zurich, 1995).
24 Jeremy Bentham, 'Manual of Political Economy, *The Works of Jeremy Bentham*, ed. John Bowring (London, 1838–43), iii. 33.
25 The classic statement remains D. O. Mannoni, *Prospero and Caliban: The Psychology of Colonization* (New York, 1956).

When Iraq invaded Kuwait in 1990, President George Bush stated that he would not allow the result to stand. His administration launched operation Desert Shield to defend Saudi Arabia, followed by operation Desert Storm to drive the Iraqi army out of Kuwait. Both succeeded, partly because the United States army limited its advance into Iraq, but mostly because the United States also limited itself to playing very effectively the role of hegemon: the crisis represents a triumph for US diplomacy rather than US military power. US troops entered Kuwait by invitation; the United Nations authorised the action and imposed sanctions against Iraq; other states vied to help either by supplying troops or by paying some of the bills; and the United States set itself the limited goal of restoring the territorial frontiers of the Middle Eastern states.[26] It aimed neither at regime change – the term used nowadays for political revolution – nor to induce a cultural revolution by exporting freedom.

Despite the United States's success in Kuwait, everything in the Middle East was not quite as it seemed. The Bush administration, by declaring Iraq to be an indirect threat to the United States, transformed it for the fourth time since the Second World War, and in Britain's imperialist manner when transforming the Middle East in 1919 and 1945. The transformation was the more surprising because the West, between 1947 and 1988, had expected Iraq to play the roles of its Middle Eastern springboard, puppet, and proxy. Until 1958, Iraq, valued for its airbases, played the role of springboard for a strategic bomber attack on the Soviet Union on the outbreak of a third world war. For the twenty-two years after the fall of the Hashemites, Iraq was expected to buttress the Northern Tier. The United States, which doubted whether the Baathist regime would prove reliable, was willing nonetheless to appease rather than destabilize it. Lastly, for nine years in the 1980s, Iraq was applauded for playing proxy for the West. It sustained at enormous cost the war aimed at destroying the Islamic republic in Iran. Once upon a time Saddam Hussein was a favourite, and favoured, US client.

The events in Kuwait show the extent to which the United States expected to turn its clients and proxies on and off like taps in high imperialist style: to copy the early nineteenth century British when dealing with the Qajar regime in Iran by giving out new parts whenever it revised the script. Between 1800 and 1837, the years of the Persian Connection when Britain was connected to the Qajar regime by treaty, the British gave seven roles to Iran.[27] They expected it to play them on cue and, when necessary, to play more than one at the same time. The first was Middle Eastern ally that would help to turn back an enemy army marching eastwards as far from India and as cheaply as possible. The second was British protectorate, the north-western outpost of British India with the Qajar dynasty ruling at Britain's direc-

---

26 Whether Iraq had legitimate territorial claims on Kuwait from the days before the partition of the Ottoman Empire remains disputed. See Peter Sluglett, 'The Resilience of a Frontier: Ottoman and Iraqi Claims to Kuwait, 1871–1990', *International History Review*, xxix (2002), 783–816.
27 Edward Ingram, *Britain's Persian Connection: Prelude to the Great Game in Asia, 1798–1828* (Oxford, 1992), pp. 5–8.

tion. The third was strategic barrier: a political no man's land in which poverty, disorder, and a fierce climate created an unbridgeable barrier. The fourth was military desert, in which British forces would advance to meet an enemy independently of the Qajar regime, as if it did not exist. The fifth was buffer state, politically stable with settled frontiers. The sixth, at the nadir of Britain's fortunes during the Napoleonic Wars after the treaty of Tilsit, was continental ally against the Franco-Russian alliance. The seventh, and perhaps ideal, was intermediary: a state that functions most effectively by increasing the varieties of relationship amongst its more powerful neighbours by giving them something to manage jointly.[28]

The transformation of Iraq from ally to indirect threat followed from developments outside, not inside, the Middle East. With the fall of the shah and the Soviet invasion of Afghanistan (which seemed to bring Soviet troops within striking range of the West's oil shipments through the straits of Hormuz; itself a nineteenth century scenario) Iraq became more valued, the role given to it more important. The dramatic implosion of the Soviet Union after the Germans pulled down the Berlin Wall lessened Iraq's importance. The circumstances seemed to be exactly opposite to those in 1956, when the Eisenhower administration claimed that the Anglo-French invasion of the Canal Zone had prevented it from trying to prevent the Soviet Union from overturning the revolution in Hungary by force. If the Soviet Union, paralyzed in Central Europe, failed to prop up its clients, the United States could risk acting openly, rather than by proxy, in the Middle East. There was no longer any need for a tournament of shadows:[29] the constraints of hegemony could be exchanged for the self-satisfactions of empire.

The invasion of Iraq in 2003 revealed the degree of the United States's drift from one towards the other. First, the United States acted unilaterally, after stating that it needed no other state's agreement when acting to ensure its own security. The George W. Bush administration, which expected the United Nations to be satisfied with the role of rubber stamp, warned any state tempted to criticize its actions to beware. Second, it declared Saddam Hussein to be a direct, not as formerly an indirect, threat to the United States. The change in status was necessary both to warrant regime change as the goal of intervention and to buttress the self image of the United States as the sole global power functioning within a unipolar system. As the British foreign secretary at end of the Napoleonic Wars, Viscount Castlereagh, told Prince Metternich when objecting to the principle underlying the Holy Alliance, only weak states fear indirect threats. Castlereagh responded to the protocol of Troppau in 1820, which stated that the great powers should act jointly to prevent regime changes in small states lest revolution should lead to war, that they should wait on each occasion to see whether a

---

28 Paul W. Schroeder, 'The Lost Intermediaries: The Impact of 1870 on the European System', *International History Review*, vi (1984), 1–27.
29 The phrase was coined by the Russian foreign minister, Count Nesselrode.

change in regime led to a change in foreign policy.[30] Only the threat of international, not domestic, instability justfied intervention: the principle on which the United States had acted in Kuwait. Thus the need both to invent (or, at least, believe in with unwarranted certainty) Iraq's weapons of mass destruction, and to align its government with terrorism, as if anyone would mistake Saddam Hussein, an old-style Middle Eastern despot, for Osama bin Laden.

The utopianism underpinning the Bush administration's invasion of Iraq was seen not merely in the speed at which the United States expected to topple the regime and to rebuild the state, but in the new role given to it. The US radical right assumed that the export of liberty and free trade to Iraq would turn its new regime into leaven working in the Middle East's Islamic dough. Iraq would become the first in a line of dominoes that, in toppling, would transform the social structures and cultural practices as well as the political systems of Middle Eastern states. Whether the development would lead Palestinians to live happily alongside Israelis was moot; it might, however, solve the problem of how to transform the Saudi regime without alienating it. Thus the radical right would not allow the oil barons, interested only in a guaranteed flow of oil at a predictable price, to make a deal with a successor authoritarian regime on the typical Middle Eastern model. Stability should come to the Middle East by the provision of order in the form of would-be Western democracy.

One wondered in 2003 how far ahead geopolitically the American radical right was looking. The United States had disagreed with its allies during the cold war about how to contain the Soviet Union in the Middle East in the way that they had not disagreed over the North Atlantic Treaty in Europe or the need to fight the Korean War. In particular they had not agreed whether Arab nationalism could be harnessed to the West's chariot or might overset it.[31] Was the invasion of Iraq a stepping stone in the bid for victory in a culture war with Islam to be fought and won before the reckoning with China? If anyone dared to risk it, given the underwriting of the US debt by Chinese capital. Or were the liberty and free trade exported to the Middle East to serve as the beacon that cast light, at last, in Far Eastern darkness, making the reckoning unnecessary? The question puzzled because the nineteenth century British, whose ideological assumptions reverberate in the Bush administration's rhetoric, dreamed not only of transforming the Middle Eastern states but also of doing so by decisively weakening Russia, seen as Britain's leading world-wide rival. The second of Britain's two attempts to weaken Russia failed owing to its apparent success; the first succeeded despite its apparent failure.

---

30   Sir Charles Webster, *The Foreign Policy of Castlereagh, 1815–1822: Britain and the European Alliance* (London, 1958), ch. 5; Paul W. Schroeder, *The Transformation of European Politics, 1793–1848* (Oxford, 1994), pp. 608–9.
31   Peter L. Hahn, *The United States, Great Britain, and Egypt, 1945–1956: Strategy and Diplomacy in the Early Cold War* (Chapel Hill and London, 1991).

Britain made a direct bid to weaken Russia on the outbreak in 1853 of the Crimean War. Palmerston dreamed of reversing more than a hundred years of Russian expansion at the expense of the Ottoman Empire by driving Russia away from the Black Sea, out of Ukraine. Russia would thus cease to be a potential Mediterranean power and Britain, deploying its seapower in the eastern Mediterranean, might undo its humiliation in 1791 during the Ochakov crisis, when it had failed to intervene effectively enough in central and eastern European affairs to back up its demand to define the territorial terms of peace between Russia and the Ottoman Empire.[32] Even though Napoleon III, who supplied the larger allied army in the Crimea, preferred to dance between Britain and Russia rather than support one exclusively at the other's expense, the terms of the peace of Paris weakened Russia in 1856 more than the extent of its defeat in the Crimea may seem to have warranted. Britain suffered however rather than benefited from the victory: Russia became relatively weaker after 1856 as a state acting with a states system, but stronger in relation to Great Britain. When Russia, neutralized in the Black Sea until 1870, sustained a forward policy in Central Asia leading to the annexation of Khiva and Bukhara, it provoked prolonged debate in Britain about the likely effect on the stability of the Indian Empire. A revolving door in which a British thrust into the Black Sea was countered by a Russian thrust towards Afghanistan, either through Khiva or Iran, might weaken Britain's worldwide geopolitical position more than Russia's.[33] It might provoke a second Mutiny in India.

The echoes in the Bush administration's rhetoric of Britain's culture war against absolutism in the Middle East originate in an indirect bid to weaken Russia by transforming the Middle East in the First Afghan War. This was the name the British gave to their invasion of Afghanistan in 1839. As Charles Trevelyan, who later replaced patronage with meritocracy in the civil service, explained to Bentinck, his patron, in 1831, Middle Easterners were eagerly awaiting the benefits of the progress bound to follow from adopting British habits. 'We shall have everything to offer them and nothing to require … We shall offer them peace, security and independence, the increase of trade and an improved condition of social life … A connection therefore which enables us to hold out the most important advantages while no sacrifice is required cannot fail to be as easily formed as, when formed, it can be productive of nothing but friendship and goodwill.'[34] In the event, the occupation of eastern Afghanistan taught the British the lesson the Bush administration is learning in Iraq: that whereas regime change is easily arranged, state building is more difficult.

---

32 For Ochakov, see Allan Cunningham, *Anglo-Ottoman Encounters in the Age of Revolution: Collected Essays, Volume One*, ed. Edward Ingram (London, 1993), chs. 1–2.

33 David Gillard, *The Struggle for Asia, 1828–1914: A Study in British and Russian Imperialism* (London, 1977), chs. 5–6.

34 'Report commercial and military upon the countries between the Caspian and the Indus by C. E. Trevelyan … and Arthur Conolly', [15–30] March 1831, [London, British Library, Oriental and] I[ndia] O[ffice Collections,] Bengal/SPC/363, 25 Nov. 1831, no. 8.

In 1838 the British declared the ruler of Kabul, Dost Muhammad Khan, to be a direct threat to Great Britain, a designation almost as puzzling as the Bush administration's similar designation of Saddam Hussein. Europeans were well aware of the results of the eighteenth-century political crises in the three most powerful Islamic empires:[35] not for more than a hundred years had an Ottoman army encamped at the gates of Vienna. The reason for the designation was Dost Muhammad's insistence on facing eastwards, towards India, and refusal to face westwards, towards Central Asia, as the British demanded. By refusing to renounce, at Britain's insistence, the territory around Peshawar he had failed, in 1834, to recapture from the Sikh confederacy that ruled in the Punjab, he presented himself as an Indian ruler likely to cause instability beyond the north-west frontier of British India. The British wished to transform him into a proxy who helped to isolate the Indian states system from the outside world. Only then could the goverment of India, bidding to control events rather than be controlled by them, act as the empire.

Britain's object in trying to persuade Dost Muhammad to face westwards, and the reason they suggested that he take Herat in replacement for Peshawar, was to pre-empt Russia in Central Asia by turning Afghanistan into a springboard. Factory-made cottons, followed by the English language and Christianity, would advance north-westwards towards Bukhara and Khiva sweeping all before them. The route through Afghanistan to Bukhara would form the second arm of a pair of geopolitical pincers that hid freedom in clothing. The first arm was the route through the Black Sea from Trabzon to Tabriz. Even a realist like Lord Ellenborough, the president of the board of control for India, the cabinet minister responsible for India, could 'not but hope [in 1830] that we might succeed in underselling the Russians and in obtaining for ourselves a large portion of at least the internal trade of Central Asia'.[36] When he read of a Russian proposal to expand Russian trade with Central Asia, he laughed: 'All this is absurd.'[37]

To suppose that freedom could be built into factory-made cottons is no more foolish, or sensible, than to suppose that one eats it along with a hamburger at Macdonald's in Moscow or drinks it from a bottle of Coca-cola in Beijing: economists exaggerate the role of status foods in bringing about cultural change. Similarly, the English language may not have proved the tool of colonial administration post-colonialists suggest and Utopians in India took for granted. Indians learned the language for their own purposes, to control one another or to limit British penetration of Indian society.[38] For Trevelyan, however, commenting in 1838 on George Macaulay's famous minute on education, written the year before, the British should 'set the natives on a process of European improvement ... Trained by us to happiness and independence, and endowed with our learning and institutions, India will remain the

---

35 C. A. Bayly, *Imperial Meridian: The British Empire and the World, 1780–1830* (London, 1989), ch. 2.
36 Secret committee to governor-general in council, 12 January 1830, IO L/PS/5/543.
37 Lord Ellenborough, *A Political Diary*, ed. Lord Colchester (London, 1881), ii. 181.
38 Eugene R. Irschick, *Dialogue and History: Constructing South India, 1795–1895* (Berkeley, 1994)

proudest monument to British benevolence.'[39] The Bush administration would say the same of Iraq.

The plan to turn Afghanistan into a springboard into Iran and Central Asia formed the last stage in a British strategy both to stabilize its territories in India and to launch its bid to pre-empt Russia's approach to the Middle Eastern coastal rimlands by opening up the Indus to British trade backed up, when necessary, by armed steamers. This strategy revealed the difficult choice to be made between local and general goals. It also asked the question whether the export of freedom would demand leverage or stand in for it. The Indus could not be opened up to trade unless the rulers of the three states along its banks – the amirs of Sind, the nawab of Bahawalpur, and the Sikh confederacy – would agree. As each made claims on the others' territory, the first requirement for success was to draw lines around all three of their states in the hope of persuading them to recognize the existing frontiers as permanent.[40]

The placement of the riverain states on the map asked, rather than answered, a second question: whether freedom along the Indus should follow from, or precede, victory in the culture war with Russia in Central Asia. If the British wished to ship goods through Sind to Afghanistan and Bukhara, they would need order in Sind, not merely stability, even if they had to depend on a typical Asian autocracy to supply it.[41] Trying to export freedom – to bring about political revolution on a liberal model, if necessary by unseating the amirs, as the prelude to the adoption by Sindians of British values and habits – would not only to cause prolonged political and social upheaval but also disrupt trade along the Indus with Afghanistan.

The British chose to prop up the amirs, temporarily, in order to focus attention on Afghanistan and Central Asia. The invasion of Afghanistan in 1839 apparently proved as successful, as quickly, and with as few casualties as the US invasion of Iraq. Dost Muhammad Khan fled to Central Asia before the British arrived at Kabul in August, leaving them to set up a new regime headed by a British puppet, Shah Shuja al-Mulk, a former ruler who had been living in exile in India. As George W. Bush announced equally prematurely of Iraq, the British seemed to have won a great victory: the road to Bukhara was open and the British leaven could begin to work on the Islamic dough. Two months later, in October, the government of India recalled most of the British troops from Kabul.[42]

39　C. E. Trevelyan, *On the Education of the People of India* (London, 1838), pp. 192–5. For Trevelyan's role in the controversy over education, see J. F. Hilliker, 'Charles Edward Trevelyan as an Educational Reformer in India', *Canadian Journal of History*, ix (1974), 275–92.

40　Edward Ingram, *The Beginning of the Great Game in Asia, 1828–1834* (Oxford, 1979), ch. 5.

41　Robert A. Huttenback, *British Relations with Sind, 1799–1843* (Berkeley, 1962).

42　The standard accounts of the Afghan War are to be found in J. A. Norris, *The First Afghan War, 1838–1842* (Cambridge, 1967), and M. E. Yapp, *Strategies of British India: Britain, Iran, and Afghanistan, 1798–1850* (Oxford, 1980). The argument here follows Edward Ingram, *Empire-building and Empire-builders* (London, 1994), ch. 9.

Increasing disorder followed, owing to Shuja's failure to stabilize his regime in the face of tribal rivalries. Instead of opening the trade route to Bukhara, his failure closed it. Shuja argued that his British advisers caused his difficulties by demanding that he rule by their notions of proper conduct. They told him to appease unruly tribes when only effective summary force would make them toe the line. Auckland prohibited the use of British troops on what he called such 'petty enterprises'.[43] But if the British demanded order in Afghanistan as well as stability, temporarily they would have to co-operate, as they had chosen to do in Sind, with a despotic regime on an Asian model that treated community as more important than liberty and the state as more important than the individual. They faced a choice of the sort the United States, perceiving a unipolar world, sees no need to make: whether to postpone the culture war against Asian superstition until they had won a victory in the cold war against European absolutism.

The British, too, refused to make the choice until forced. After Shah Shuja warned the British garrison of Kabul in the autumn of 1841 that he could no longer ensure its safety, Auckland decided to withdraw it. The result was one of Britain's most notorious humiliations: the loss of 4,000 troops and 12,000 camp followers during the retreat to Jalalabad ranks with Yorktown, Isandalwhana, and Kut. The comparison is less misleading than it appears. Yorktown led to the loss of thirteen of Britain's North-American colonies. The retreat from Kabul had no repurcussions in India; nor did it prevent the British from reaching one of the two goals they had set themselves in Afghanistan. But just as victory at Yorktown might not have ensured the success of Britain's bid to prevent the loss of the American colonies, a better managed retreat to Jalalabad would not have disguised Britain's setback in its culture war in Central Asia.

If the victory turned out to be false, the same could be said of the defeat. The British had not withdrawn their forces elsewhere in Afghanistan. They were keen to show that they had not, and would not, leave Afghanistan under duress.[44] In September 1842, the Army of Retribution marched back to Kabul, to be joined there by a force from Kandahar. They burned down the bazaar before leaving Shuja al-Mulk to his fate; defeat by Dost Muhammad. The British settled for stable disorder among a group of small Afghan states instead of the stable order in a large Afghan state they needed for their culture war. They made the choice because Dost Muhammad, on taking back the throne, agreed to the demand they had made of him: he turned westwards. Even during the Crimean War and the Indian Mutiny, when he had every opportunity to take advantage of Britain's difficulties by trying to recover the lost territory in the Punjab, he held aloof beyond the Hindu Kush.

---

43 Auckland to Hobhouse, private, 16 February 1840, British Library, Add. MSS 36 474, fo. 229.
44 Cf. the last chapter of Linda Colley, *Captives: Britain, Empire, and the World, 1600–1850* (London, 2002), which advances the Victorian argument that the British went back to Afghanistan to rescue hostages.

The recent regime changes in Afghanistan and Iraq suggest that the international system is reapplying the principles underpinning the Vienna settlement. The politicians and diplomats who met at the congress of Vienna not only remapped Europe to wipe out the Napoleonic Empire but also stipulated how states should conduct themselves in different parts of the world. First, they marked off the core of the system from the periphery. They defined the core, on cultural grounds, as central and western Europe. The Ottoman Empire, one of the two largest European states, was explicitly excluded: the protections the Final Act of the congress of Vienna afforded to other European states did not apply to it. Within the core, the Vienna settlement required states to act multi-laterally under the unipolar umbrella of the concert of Europe. Although the settlement recognized a role for regional hegemony within the alliance – for Austria in Italy, Britain in the Low Countries, and Russia in Poland – the alliance prohibited bids to act the role of empire.[45]

Outside the core, in the periphery, which began in the Ottoman Balkans and extended throughout the Middle East, the opposite rules applied. The wider world was treated as multi-polar, and unilateral actions were tolerated there of the sort prohibited in the core. The outcome was bellicist empire-building by Russia in the Middle East, Britain in the Middle East and India, and France in the Middle East and North Africa. The difference between the Vienna system and the assumptions underpinning the foreign policy of the George W. Bush administration, lies in the United States's unwillingness to distinguish between periphery and core. The core is the United States: everywhere else is the periphery. Member states of the European Union, such as Germany and France when they protest against the proposed invasion of Iraq, are addressed as if they were peripheral puppets rather than established allies; Canada, like Afghanistan and Iraq, is expected to play whatever role the United States decides to give to it. The implosion of the Soviet Union led too many Americans to see the world as unipolar. This development is either seen to be the result of the victory of liberal capitalism or gives liberal capitalism the opportunity for victory that the United States should seize. The US bid to transform Afghanistan and Iraq becomes a stepping stone from geopolitical victory to universal peace.

The intellectual underpinning of this claim is provided by democratic peace theory. According to American political science, democracies supposedly are more peaceable than autocracies. One would never guess this from observing the conduct of the United States, which supplies evidence for the theory's refined version: that democracies are less likely than autocracies to go to war with similar sorts of states, if no less likely to go to war with autocracies. The implication is that such bellicist conduct is unavoidable; a contagion likely to be caught as long as autocracies continue to exist.

Like much political science, democratic peace theory hinges on definitions; on the sorts of actions that count as war and the sorts of states that meet the test of being democratic. It

---

45 Edward Ingram, *The British Empire as a World Power* (London, 2001), ch. 5.

fails to take account of the United States's twenty-year long attack on Great Britain, which culminated in 1956, because their troops seemed to fight on the same side in the Second World War.[46] To count as democratic the German Empire, which threatened France with war in 1905 during the Moroccan crisis, and also Great Britain, which threatened it with war in 1898 during the Fashoda crisis, turns the early twentieth century international system into a more bellicist refinement of the Vienna system: Germany during the Moroccan crisis and again during the Bosnian crisis threatened another European state with war in the core in an attempt to promote its empire-building in the periphery. In Keith Wilson's words, the First World War was a war between everyone against everyone else in pursuit of world power.[47]

The events in Kuwait, Afghanistan, and Iraq contradict the George W. Bush adminstration's claim that the United States has the capability to act as the empire and need not recognize the capabilities of other states nor accept the constraints of hegemony. The United States's willingness to act as the hegemon when organizing the defence of Kuwait and the overthrow of the Taliban forestalled the likelihood of balancing by other states instead of bandwagoning. Its conduct in Iraq provoked the opposite response. Its difficulty in state building, in promoting stable order rather than aggravating the disorder or leaving the inhabitants to fight it out, need not surprise. The Bush administration needs more help than it will admit in waving its 'big stick'.

Five unacknowledged demands for help in Iraq illustrate the limits to the United States's capability to project limited, but decisive, military power world-wide. The decision, under duress, to base the headquarters of the US Central Command, responsible for the Middle East, in Florida is evidence of political difficulty as much as military capability. The first need was a Middle Eastern parking lot; somewhere at which to deploy the US troops ahead of the invasion. Kuwait offered one; Saudi Arabia, notably, did not. The second need was for a springboard. Turkey was asked to open its air space to US bombers, to enable them to attack Iraq from the west, and to open a corridor from the Mediterranean to the Iraq border for US supply trains. The US bombers could not attack Iraq from the east without the use of the base at Diego Garcia in the Indian Ocean that Britain had built for them when Jimmy Carter created the US 5th Fleet, now based at Bahrein, in 1979. The third need was for sidekicks; other states willing to supply infantry, partly in the hope of limiting the number of US casualties, partly because US troops, the most highly trained and best equipped for battle, are less than ideally suited to peacekeeping. The fourth need was for a begging bowl; passed around among other states in search of contributions towards the cost of reconstruction. While the United States limited itself to the role of hegemon, restoring the established Middle Eastern order in Kuwait, and leading the grand alliance against terrorism in Afghanistan (even if the

---

46 Wm. Roger Louis, *Imperialism at Bay: The United States and the Decolonization of the British Empire, 1941–1945* (New York, 1978); Christopher G. Thorne, *Allies of a Kind: The United States, Britain, and the War against Japan* (London, 1978).
47 Keith Wilson, *Problems and Possibilities: Exercises in Statesmanship, 1814–1918* (Stroud, 2003), ch. 18.

regime change required the transformation of the Taliban from proxy in the cold war into sponsor of terrorism), large numbers of states followed its lead. When the Bush administration acted unilaterally, most of them held aloof.

The last and most revealing need was for sheriff's deputies, as Australia called itself: someone to mind the store in other parts of the world while the United States focussed its attention on the Middle East. Australia's task, apart from supplying troops in a gesture of political solidarity, was to monitor events in Indonesia, the political heart of Islam and a more likely seedbed of terrorism than Saddam Hussein's Iraq. Britain's task was spoiler in the European Union: to make sure that 'old Europe', as Donald Rumsfeld called France and Germany, did not seduce the Union's new members with the siren-song of post-Gaullist anti-Americanism.

There has been prolonged debate in the United States about whether, given its shortage of troops, it is capable of handling two major crises at the same time; especially if it applies the Powell doctrine of deploying sufficient force to ensure victory without delay or heavy losses. One hears an echo of the debate in Britain in 1832 about whether the admiralty could deploy a second fleet in the eastern Mediterranean to defend Mahmud II against Mehemet Ali while the Mediterranean fleet was supporting constitutionalists against absolutists in Portugal. Six years later, between 1838 and 1842, and notwithstanding its setbacks in Afghanistan, Britain gave a demonstration of hegemonic world power that radical right supporters of the George W. Bush administration should envy. It deployed expeditionary forces in Argentina, in the eastern Mediterranean to help to drive Mehemet Ali out of Syria, in the Persian Gulf to nullify his empire-building in Arabia, in southern Iran to compel the shah to break off the siege of Herat, and in China to sustain Britain's honour and prestige (as Palmerston described the Opium War).[48] Meantime, the government of India, while invading Afghanistan, was keeping tabs on the Sikh confederacy in the Punjab, and fending off Nepal in the north-east and Burma in the south-east. By the end of the crisis, Britain had weakened France's influence in the Middle East by confining its proxy, Mehemet Ali, to Egypt. It had weakened Russia's influence by the terms of the convention of London of 1841. By prohibiting the Russian warships from travelling from the Black Sea into the Mediterranean while the Ottoman Empire was at peace, the treaty nullified Russia's claim to hegemony in the Middle East. Henceforth hegemony would be shared and the Ottoman Empire would play the role of intermediary.

The George W. Bush administration's dissatisfaction with the constraints of hegemony and attraction to empire arises partly from the self-fulfilling prophecy of the Powell doctrine. The bigger the build-up envisaged, the bigger the threat to be met. The United States magnified the threat from Iraq without sending enough troops to have a chance of winning the political battle that followed its decisive victory over Saddam Hussein's army. The Powell

---

48 Glenn Melancon, *Britain's China Policy and the Opium Crisis: Balancing Drugs, Violence, and National Honour, 1833–1840* (Aldershot, 2003).

doctrine, admired for its emphasis on an exit strategy, turns out to be Utopian in its assumption that, so long as the United States plans correctly, it is able to control eventualities. Britain had made the same mistake in Egypt; and a similar supposition underpinned the Schlieffen plan. The only exit strategy bound to work is one modelled on Britain's strategy in India in 1947: the announcement of a decision to partition the Indian Empire on a given date regardless of the disorder and deaths bound to follow. Britain, however, had succeeded until the Second World War in isolating the Indian Empire from events in the wider world; even Hitler refused to seek Middle Eastern allies in a bid to destabilize it.[49]

The United States aggravates its difficulties in the Middle East by using the rhetoric of the empire even when satisfied with the role of hegemon. The rhetoric, which offends foreigners, is tailored to a domestic audience. Truman insisted in 1947 that Americans would not sign up for the Atlantic alliance until the administration had given them a fright. Telling the efficient from the decorative components of foreign policy becomes more difficult when a state has to wrap up all of its decisions in statements of principle. Outsiders cannot tell what matters to it most; or when they should appease it and when they may safely resist. The same complaint was made of British foreign policy in the 1880s under Gladstone and Earl Granville.[50]

British politicians are often mocked for their fondness for the 'special relationship' with the United States. They look back to the Second World War when Harold Macmillan dreamed of Britain's playing civilized Greece to the United States's uncouth Rome. But Britain does have such a relationship, though not the one British politicians imagine. The Bush administration pays little more attention to Tony Blair than to any other European politician on a visit to Washington unless he sings from the song sheet it supplies. The special relationship derives from the emergence of the Anglosphere; from the geopolitical fact that the new, post cold war, American empire is built on the relicts of the old British one: Canada, the United Kingdom, Egypt (at vast expense in aid) Pakistan (though not usually India), Australia, and Japan (on the list because of the crucial role it played for Britain which, in 1901, did not see how to meet the challenges expected in the Far East without its help).[51]

In the middle of this formerly seaborne, and now airborne, ring around continental Eurasia lies the Middle Eastern gap, one Britain tried to close by answering the Eastern Question and playing the Great Game in Asia. Finding a way to close the gap gave the post-Second World War United States as much trouble as it gave nineteenth-century Great Britain. Hence the siren song of the culture war with its claims to be able to hurdle geopolitical obstacles

---

49 Milan Hauner, *India in Axis Strategy: Germany, Japan, and Indian Nationalists in the Second World War* (Stuttgart, 1981).
50 See the introduction to *The Political Correspondence of Mr Gladstone and Lord Granville, 1876–1886*, ed. Agatha Ramm (Oxford, 1962).
51 Robert J. McMahon, *The Cold War on the Periphery: The United States, India, and Pakistan* (New York, 1994); Ian H. Nish, *The Anglo-Japanese Alliance: The Diplomacy of Two Island Empires, 1894–1907* (2nd edition, London, 1985).

easily and quickly. And hence the peregrinations of Condoleeza Rice, whose forthright tones when addressing foreigners carry an overtone of petulance that hints at disappointment. Aren't other people (especially Muslims?) strange? But they *do* want to be like us. They *must* want to. We shall allow them to search for freedom in their own way because their idea of freedom is *our* idea and their way doubtless will be *our* way. But if they have another idea and choose another way?

Was the Middle-East the Birthplace of a Common European Foreign Policy?

Alan S. Milward

The initial wavering steps taken by the European Economic Community (EEC) towards discussion of a common 'European' foreign policy can be seen in the meeting in Munich in 1970 of European Political Cooperation (EPC). Such meetings, at first of foreign secretaries or professional diplomats, were not included in the bureaucratic organigram of the Community and thus without any standard form of procedures which could bring their discussions within the bureaucratic framework of the European Commission. Diplomats dealt directly with other diplomats, no doubt with a close eye to the likelihood of an expansion of the EEC in mind.

When the Luxembourg Report on the possibilities of a more unified European Community came for discussion at the Paris summit meeting of 19/20 October 1972, after the agreed extension of membership to the UK, Denmark and Ireland, the heads of state asserted their firm intention to proceed with the development of the EEC into an eventual European Monetary Union. For that purpose, they doubled the number of EPC meetings at ministerial level to four meetings annually of the foreign ministers of the member-states, who were directed to produce a further report on ways of improving the functioning of EPC in conformity with the Luxembourg Report. EPC remained, however, an institution separate from the European Commission. This was only to change officially with the Maastricht Treaty in 1991–2 and the agreement to proceed with Economic and Monetary Union (EMU). This step led to the incorporation of a further discussion group, Common Foreign and Security Policy (CFSP), into the bureaucratic framework of the supranation.

Why in this perspective is the common European foreign policy so often attributed to the early 1970s? Foreign ministers of member-states were asked to draw up a report on what a common foreign policy might involve. Their contribution became the 'Copenhagen Report' of July 1973, a document stronger on rhetoric than on the details of political change. Its existence, however, did play a part when late in 1974 the European Council, the regular meeting of heads of state and government which was foreseen as a decision-taking body in the expanding Community, became the formal decision-taking body for EPC. This seems a small change, but it was one which for the future at least established intra-state cooperation in the foreign policy responses of the future European Union (EU), including security policies, any discussion of which had so far been more or less a taboo within the Community.

What led to this change? Its political basis was of course the accession of the United Kingdom into the European Community, the only member-state with armed power and with an empire in both cases as extensive as France's power and influence outside its own boundaries. This was what France's President Georges Pompidou had deemed necessary if the Community was to be expanded. His views and those of the UK Prime Minister, Edward Heath, were set out in the official record of their personal negotiations. «The President of the Republic and the British Prime Minister established that their views on the role and development of Europe were in all essentials identical.» ... «They further agreed that the French and British governments would work together to develop a distinctive European personality in world affairs with distinctive European policies which will recognise and give expression to the common interests of Europe principally in economic affairs but also more generally.»[1]

Such lavish language summed up the mood. The previous decade of American tergiversation in foreign policy towards Western Europe had driven British ministers and diplomats increasingly towards the nearer shore. The UK by 1971 was in favour of developing a common foreign policy within the European Community. It was perhaps even more interested in developing with France a common defence policy, but there the exaggerated language with which the two countries celebrated their agreement was reduced to reality. President Pompidou remained as Gaullist as the general whose successor he was. He would not accept any discussion of a common defence policy in the long negotiating sessions with Heath. Indeed, he expressly asked Heath not to raise the topic. France's nuclear «force de frappe» was sacrosanct as long as de Gaulle and the Gaullist Party survived in sufficient force to keep it so.

Only, therefore, with a major omission could the Franco-British agreement on UK entrance to the EEC be construed as a new regime for governing unified Europe, if that regime was confined to the political direction of the future European Union. If economic policy changes are taken into account, however, the Franco-British rapprochement could be construed as having a more comprehensive influence on the original member-states of the EEC. The greater readiness of the member-states to tolerate a regime dominated by the two greater powers in the Community, albeit that the Netherlands maintained a strong disagreement with such an outcome, is more understandable if a full view is taken of the expansion of the Common Market. Denmark, Ireland and Norway would enter the Common Market on the same day as the United Kingdom, although in the event Norwegians voted against entry. France proposed and the United Kingdom accepted the replacement of the Yaoundé Conventions, which were the model for Community trade and aid to the former French

---

1 National Archives of the UK (henceforward, NA), FCO 30/1152, Record of the Conclusions of the Meetings between the President of the French Republic and the Prime Minister of the United Kingdom held at Le Palais de l'Elysée, Paris, 20/21 May, 1971.

empire, by more far-reaching and flexible arrangements under a new framework, the Lomé Conventions signed in 1975, which would further standardize trade, aid and tariff rules throughout both empires. Both 'empires' included all other territorial dependencies including newly-independent countries, even those in the Caribbean and the Pacific. Forty-six countries would thus be added to the list of the Community's adherents to common trade rules. By 2002 that increased number had grown to 78. Almost the entirety of their exports by value went to the Common Market. In this light the expansion of the Community went well beyond the imposition of the *acquis communautaire* on the three new Community member-states.

So large an expansion gave the EC a world presence, amplified by its Mediterranean Programme, which regulated EC trade with the Mediterranean littoral. Economically, this presence did not match the initial hopes. Volumes and values with trade of the underdeveloped countries remained distressingly small. From the Community's viewpoint, the Lomé Conventions remained nationally designed and administered, the Commission's input being strictly limited by changing French and British policies towards the individual receivers of aid.

Even so, the rule of Community preference for goods traded within the Community, which the UK had to accept, and the parallel rule that Community preference should also be available to goods from the states which had signed the Lomé accords constituted an unwelcome challenge from Washington's point of view. The EEC was seen from Washington as displacing American primary exports to the British market. A spectacular increase in the value of intra-Community commerce began in 1970. The EU's share of total world trade by value rose over the period 1970 to 2000 to 41.4 per cent of world imports. The expansion of the Community had started the process by which the Common Market of the EC/EU was to become the world's biggest market.

However, the widening and deepening of the Community is not ascribable to a Franco-British domination of the Community and a re-writing of its rules by the two nations. While Pompidou and his ministers sought to retain France's role as influential it had been in the six-member EEC, the gate through which the UK entered into membership was strait. The *acquis communautaire*, which the UK had to accept in full, was intended to demonstrate that Pompidou's persistence with the European Community as a basis for a global French foreign policy would be sustained, rather than changed, by British membership. Pompidou was fortunate that Heath was ready to meet most of those terms and that Heath thought the Community likely to be more supportive of UK foreign and economic policy than was the USA.

The conviviality and enthusiasm at the close of the Franco-British negotiations did not endure. Michel Jobert, director of Pompidou's cabinet when he was prime minister (1966–8) and Secretary-General of the Presidency (1969–73) when Pompidou was President, a key figure in the Anglo-French negotiations, tried to make Franco/British cooperation within the Community more durable. He sought, but failed, to convince Pompidou that by appointing leading political figures to serve for one year as internationally respected symbols of the Community, the directions which France and Britain had together taken could be safeguarded and their cooperation strengthened. Willy Brandt would be the first such living symbol in 1974, Heath would be the second in 1975, and Pompidou himself in 1976. Pompidou declined the personal role and did not support Jobert's proposal. Men, he told Jobert, were less durable than institutions.[2] He knew of what he spoke. He died in 1974 of cancer. Charles de Gaulle had died in 1970. Edward Heath, having taken Britain into the European Community, lost the general election, which he himself called, in February 1974, and never reappeared as a major political figure in the UK or the EC. France was left to watch and lament Britain's return to closer attachment to American leadership under Heath's successor as leader of the Conservative Party and Prime Minister, Margaret Thatcher. As for the symbolic figures, Pompidou was justified in his rejection of the idea by opposition from the smaller member-states.

The idea of such foreign-policy discussion tables as EPC and then CFSP did, however, find more sympathy in Paris. Pompidou at the Hague Summit in 1969 spoke of the possibility of creating something more official along the lines of CFSP, although rather vaguely. EPC was supported by France as one aspect of 'deepening', but France was firm in its insistence that there should be a clear barrier line between the Community, including the Commission, on the one side and the international diplomatic discussions between states within the shelter of the Community on the other.

The subsequent erosion of that barrier line has been explained by the allegedly strong bureaucratic propensity of international institutions to path dependency. In the case of EPC and later of CFSP the implication is that both organisations would increasingly shape themselves to the task of pursuing the objective of a Community-wide foreign policy stance. It would become their agenda, because the task of pursuing the integration of western Europe was the central task of the European Community, however strongly French governments might believe that such a trajectory would weaken France's national dominance in shaping and preserving the foreign policy purpose of the supranational political machinery. The conviction of so much political science in the 1960s that European integration was the culmination of functionalist political ideas and practices of the inter-war period elevated the concept of «spillover» as a driving consequence of such ideas. Spillover featured strongly in supporting the idea that any form of international agreement on practical cooperation on political issues of a lower level of importance was not only a triumph of functionalist practicality, marking an inbuilt trend towards something larger, political integration itself, whence the ease of reaffirming that international institutions would be path-dependent, that supposition in its turn helping functionalist theory to envisage the destiny of the path as integra-

---

2   Michel Jobert, *Memoires d'avenir*, (Paris, Bernard Grasset, 1974) pp. 253-4. On Edward Heath's private acquaintance with Jobert see Edward Heath, *The Course of My Life* (Hodder and Stoughton, London, 1998) pp. 361, 365-374.

tion, economic and political.[3] One can readily understand the unease of the US State Department over the trajectory, whether theoretical or real, of a single Europe with a single foreign policy.

There are other and now more fashionable explanations of the tendency of EC/EU institutions to stand together on issues of foreign policy. Argumentative entrapment, deriving from the inevitability of having to make some statement about internal and external problems or intentions to the rest of the Community, is seen by many commentators as a pressure towards collective involvement in foreign affairs. If it were not so, the driving force would be economic, the size of the Common Market and its mercantile power meant that trade was the one aspect of an integrated Europe to which the world had to listen when the Community spoke.

It is in that light that the USA had to question whether the integration of Europe, which Washington had in 1945–1950 first helped and encouraged as the best way forward to concluding a durable peace, might not in the 1960s weaken America's position both in Europe and elsewhere on the globe. The Copenhagen Report, with its sturdy description of what a European policy on the Middle East might be, offered no comfort to Washington. It was a reflection of the division of opinion on the Middle East between Europe and the USA which still persists.

To explain British acceptance of the Copenhagen Report, it is perhaps not necessary to look to an institutionalized bureaucracy nor to any of the other bureaucratic tendencies of the European Commission. New type of institutional development that it was, the European Community was as vulnerable as any more familiar state-form to the pressures arising from the habitual, unanticipated disturbances of international relations. The Report generated an enduring, albeit skeletal, common understanding of foreign policy in the Middle East, that the Community had to take up the same international tasks as did unitary nation-states, while at the same time proclaiming itself as the model for the replacement of the nation-state. The Copenhagen Report represented the evolution of a common policy emerging as a common response to truly dangerous trends and events outside supranational Europe which imperilled the Community's overall policies as urgently and decisively as any trends which developed within the effort to make the European Community function *less* like a nation-state.

An interesting question runs throughout the fabric of earlier work by David Allen, who leant towards the argument that threats from outside the Community played their part in sustaining the progress of EPC towards a more comprehensive framework of foreign policy, more so than did the institutionalisation of Community discussion and the path-depen-

---

3   Michael E. Smith, *Europe's Foreign and Security Policy. The Institutionalization of Cooperation*. Cambridge University Press, Cambridge, 2004. "However, it is also clear that the specific institutional reforms of EU foreign policy resulting from these events largely reflected endogenous path-dependent processes." p. 176.

dency of its institutions.[4] The opposite view is well represented in the work of Thomas Risse-Kappen, for whom any institution which must react to trends in the foreign policy of foreigners will be the perfect example of argumentative entrapment, for it exists to feed such converse.[5] A more direct link to national foreign policies is made by the collective work edited by Christopher Hill.[6] It contains an interesting discussion of how far the Community's emergent common foreign policy was a direct outcome of Community expansion intended to retain and support the position which the EC held and its purpose. Françoise de la Serre and Philippe Moreau Desfarges, reviewing the same issue within French foreign policy, illustrate the difficulties of such a policy in a period when widening had been thought of as a necessary step if the Community was to be preserved.[7]

Neither the child of a new Entente Cordiale nor the helpless orphan of argumentative entrapment, for what purposes did the Community exist? This is a question that must be answered to answer the titular question. If the Community was threatened externally, what was the threat? The first answer must be that the links with the USA arising from France's determination to build, and then preserve, in Germany a democratic state with which, no matter how long it took, a comprehensive peace treaty could be negotiated and signed by the victors of the Second World War, France, the USA and the UK. For twenty post-war years it had looked unattainable, but the pariah amongst the victors had begun publicly to invite changes to attitudes to Germany. The proposal made by the USSR, through the auspices of the Warsaw Pact, on 17 March 1969 for a conference on European Security and Cooperation which, among other objectives, would include recognising the inviolability of all European frontiers, including Poland's post-war frontier with Germany, the Oder-Neisse line, was the first real intimation that a peace treaty might be reached. The inviolability of the Oder-Neisse line seemed to imply either the German Federal Republic (BRD) standing ready to abandon its aspiration to represent all Germans and the territories in which they lived or a merger of the two post-war German states.

Less than a year earlier however talks between Sir Dennis Greenhill, Head of the British Diplomatic Service, and Mr S. P. Kozyrev, the Soviet Minister of Foreign Trade and Deputy Minister of Foreign Affairs, on 23 January 1968 had been sufficiently amicable for British diplomats to suppose that the long-awaited peace treaty with Germany might not be so far away. The obvious problem was that there had been almost no discussion as yet of the future

4   David Allen, Reinhardt Rummel, and Wolfgang Wessels (eds.), *European Political Cooperation: Towards a Foreign Policy for Western Europe*, Butterworths, London: 1982. The volume contains an essay by David Allen and William Wallace, "European Political Cooperation: The Historical and Contemporary Background" which directly raises the same question.
5   Thomas Risse-Kappen (ed.), *Bringing Transnational Relations Back In: Non-State Actors, Domestic Structures and International Institutions* (Cambridge University Press, 1995).
6   Christopher Hill (ed.), *National Foreign Policies and European Political Cooperation* (London, George Allen and Unwin, 1983).
7   Françoise de la Serre and Philippe Moreau Desfarges, "France: A Penchant for Leadership" in Christopher Hill (London, 1983) comment pertinently on how durable French leadership could really be.

of Berlin.[8] What effect a peace treaty would have on the European Economic Union was also left unclear. The background to Community widening was thus already one of impending change, before the terms of widening might be accepted.

At the same time the expanded Community was face to face with another threat, the renewal of Arab-Israeli armed conflict in the Middle East and, as a consequence, the imposition by the Arabs of differentiated oil embargoes on the European Community member-states and the USA. The embargo was seen in Britain as a dangerous potential blow to the UK's balance of payments, the weakness of which in the 1960s had fortified French opposition to British EC membership and now, in 1969, seemed to indicate that British entry into the Economic and Monetary Union would be dangerous to the Community's ambitions. American foreign policy showed no tendency to strengthen the European Union by strengthening the UK pound on the exchanges. Its attitudes to the European Community and to the UK were of indifference verging on hostility.

That the USA had taken upon itself the role of patron to Israel meant that the EC would be inevitably involved in an ambiguous relationship with the USA's policy towards the Middle East and the Mediterranean, to say nothing of American hostile reactions to the spread of the Common Market's trade agreements to the northern littoral of the Mediterranean as well as to its treaty links with the Arab world. The Copenhagen Report has to be construed as a declaration of independence of the Community's *commercial* policy. It was accepted as such by Heath's government in part because of the contradictory and wavering policies of the USA towards Britain and the Community, particularly Henry Kissinger's ambivalence about the noisily proclaimed «Year of Europe». Furthermore, the Soviet Union's proposal for a European security conference was at first treated unenthusiastically by the USA, in part because of the Soviet-American tensions over events in the Middle East. The US government feared the increase of the Soviet Union's influence there. The British response to the Soviet proposal, while not friendly, assumed that it reflected the weakness, rather than the danger, of the Soviet Union in the Middle East, particularly the loss of prestige which the failure of Soviet attempts to broker a peace settlement in the region imposed.

The «Six Day War» in June 1967 at first threatened Israel's hold on its eastern and north-eastern frontiers. Its outcome, however, was the loss of Arab territory to Israel through its seizure of the Golan Heights, while at the same time the Israeli hold on Sinai as a defensive position was strengthened. In that situation the view of the USSR that a peace settlement depended on Israel withdrawing to its former boundaries could only encounter rejection in Washington. In talks with Sir Alec Douglas-Home, the UK Secretary for Foreign Affairs, the Soviet Minister for Foreign Affairs, Andrei Gromyko, pressed for a resumption of the one effort which had been agreed towards a peace settlement, the establishment of the former Swedish Ambassador to the USSR, Gunnar Jarring, in the post of Special Representative of

---

8 G. Bennett and K. A. Hamilton (eds.), *Documents on British Policy Overseas*, Series III Volume 1 (London, The Stationery Office, 1997), p. 219, Document No. 45.

the Secretary General of the United Nations on the Middle-Eastern question. Part of Jarring's task was to restore the pre-1967 boundaries of Palestine and to prolong the ceasefire, otherwise due to expire on 5 November in a week's time. Douglas-Home's reply was that only the USA could persuade Israel to withdraw, although he maintained the view that UN Security Council Resolution No. 242, which required Israeli withdrawal from the occupied territories, and which Washington rejected, should be the basis of a peace settlement.

The USA was primarily concerned to reach a settlement which would make the Soviet Union's position in the Middle East even more marginal than it had become. Seven months after the ceasefire had halted the Six-Day War, about eight hundred Israeli settlers had by then made homes for themselves in the West Bank, which had been seized by and was still controlled by the Israeli army.[9] This has to be measured seen against the fact that in the 1948 war, which secured Israel's status as an independent nation, the war left intact about 78 per cent of the territorial area of the former UN mandate of Palestine. UN policy was still specifically aimed at guaranteeing the security of frontiers, but the issue that was avoided was who would live in safety within those frontiers. Interpreted, as it seemed, by Israel's army and by the new wave of settlement which the army encouraged as a way of making the *de facto* frontier of Israel more secure, there appeared little chance of agreement on a peace settlement between Israel and the Arab states which would not seriously increase the future dangers for Europe in the Middle East, not least by an inevitable weakening of UK-USA relationships and the lack of agreement between the UK and the USA in talks on the Security Treaty.

The Soviet Union's influence in the Middle East probably reached its lowest point as it became evident that the enforcement of the UN Security Council's requirements to bring about a settlement of the Arab/Israeli problem was only possible if the USA shared the UN's position. It did not do so. The Soviet response to the USA's attitude was to increase its naval strength in the Mediterranean, to support the Arab states in the United Nations and to re-arm them. Britain had proclaimed its neutrality in the brief war of 1967. Its interests in the Middle East were, though, active and vital. The prime interest was freedom of navigation in the area, notably for the shipment of oil. For that, good relationships with the Arabs were also a necessity. In an Arab perspective, however, the UK was too closely tied to the USA to influence American policy in the Mediterranean and Middle East.

Seen from London, the lack of progress towards a peace agreement threatened Britain's oil supply from the Arab world. For the USA, as seen from London, the lack of a general peace agreement was an outcome which American-owned oil companies were unlikely to regret. The history of the nationalisation of the Anglo-Iranian oil company in the 1950s and the related increase in US resources in Iran still rankled. Waiting for another US-brokered settlement seemed to mean accepting not only every advantage which Israel and the USA took from the situation, but also inviting a greater degree of Arab hostility to Britain.

---

9   Gershom Gorenberg, *The Accidental Empire. Israel and the Birth of the Settlements*, 1967-1977 (Times Books, New York, 2006).

In the Middle East, the USSR and France pressed for the detailed drafting of guidelines for Jarring, while Britain, in common with the USA, disagreed with such a step. Their agreement to disagree was, however, under increasing pressure. On 8 January 1970 Michael Stewart, the UK Foreign Secretary, wrote to the prime minister that Britain should refrain from making any definite proposals about a peace settlement in the Middle East in order to «avoid being forced to choose between accepting or rejecting language which the Americans could not accept, that is to choose between isolating the Americans or appearing to agree with them on subjects where our real position does not coincide with theirs».[10]

Kozyrev envisaged a settlement with Israel in the context of the European Security Conference. Sir Denis Greenhill's apparent goodwill and sincerity in awkward sessions with Kozyrev on 7 April paved the way for a more focussed and frank meeting with him and his team at the Foreign and Commonwealth Office in the course of which the UK's interest in a European Security Conference was made evident, with no mention of American attitudes.

The retirement of General de Gaulle in April 1969 from the Presidency of France, followed by the Hague summit at the start of December, made things easier. The summit called for consideration of 'political unification' of the European Economic Community. These instructions were passed to the Political Directors of the six EC foreign ministries. The Political Directors had their place because they were the barrier on which the French had initially insisted between the Community and EPC. It was they, under the chairmanship of their Belgian colleague, Etienne Davignon, who established EPC as a first step towards a common European foreign policy, by taking away the French barrier.

The journey from not being officially recognised as constructors of a common policy which effectively distinguished European attitudes from American is to be ascribed in part to the lack of clarity and decision in American attitudes to the growing commercial power of the Common Market and in part to the need to cope with genuine threats to Western European security in Europe from events in the Middle East as well as in the European continent itself. The international status of Davignon's report as a text was furthered by the perception that threats to the post-1945 European settlement were feared by east and west Europe alike and particularly so when they originated in the Middle East. Writing to Michael Stewart, the Foreign Secretary, on 28 March 1969 the UK ambassador to Moscow, Sir D. Wilson, expressed himself as follows:

If HMG considered objectively the question of settlement of the Middle East crisis it should be clear that in this context Britain and the Soviet Union should be moving in the same direction. The Middle East situation was fraught with danger. The closure of the Suez Canal was both economically and financially damaging not only to the Soviet Union and to Britain but to many other countries. The Soviet Government's position was well known to HMG. It

---

10 G. Bennett and K. A. Hamilton, *Documents on British Policy Overseas*, Series III Volume 1. Britain and the Soviet Union, 1968-1972 (London, The Stationery Office, 1997), p. 223, footnote 13.

believed in a just settlement for both sides, which would guarantee the security of both Israel and the Arab States. HMG would gain positive capital in the world by pursuing a similarly constructive policy. Britain and the Soviet Union should be more active in seeking together a settlement.[11]

When Israel did not change its tactics by mid-March 1970 and Soviet planes and missiles had been deployed to Egypt. Israel was reassured by Washington that the USA would ensure a military balance in Israel's favour. Wilson's and Stewart's caution had not made the world safer for Britain. All British political and economic interests in the Middle East appeared to be facing rejection in a more widespread and violent struggle. Britain turned cautiously back to the USSR. In early April Mr Kozyrev, the Soviet Deputy Minister of Foreign Affairs, was asked by British diplomats for his thoughts on the still unachieved Jarring mission, and on the Russian/American talks on arms limitation. He make it clear in his reply that Britain should influence Israel to take «a more realistic position about a settlement».[12]

At the apex of policy was the compulsion to overcome any and every threat to obtaining the eventual four-power treaty with Germany. To fail in this would be every bit as dangerous to the purpose of the European Community, whether the threat came from within Europe or from the Middle East. In this light the origins of the common foreign policy sprang from the need to defend the Community from serious threats to its existence and purpose, threats from which the institutionalization of the Community also drew its strength but at levels which had become less important. Britain had little choice other than to push for a stronger European role in the Middle East, as the Soviet diplomats insisted, but that was precisely what Britain was in no position to do.

There was only one call from the USA for Israel to withdraw from its territorial gains, the appeal by the US Secretary of State William Rogers on 9 December 1969. It went unheeded. In other areas the USA was not helpful. When the pound was pushed by financial pressures out of the embryonic monetary union of the Community, the USA gave it no support, even as President Pompidou was saying that the UK must be in the European currency system. The «Year of Europe», proposed and orchestrated by Henry Kissinger, did not help Europe in any shape or form, his discontent with the European Community was frequently expressed. In the Arab perspective the UK was too closely tied to the USA to influence American policy in the Mediterranean and the Middle East. The USA was uncertain that a settlement in Europe was safer for its purposes than the ability to use its leverage over Israel. By contrast, Douglas-Home thought that without a Middle Eastern settlement Arab turbulence would reassert itself. It was he who argued strongly inside the government for the way to an agreement with the Arabs, including greater generosity of aid and ready sales of weapons, except in the case of those which were banned by agreements with the United Nations. These

11 *Ibid.*, p. 124, Document No. 26.
12 *Ibid.*, p. 224, footnote 15.

ideas were brought into one package when the Arab threat to embargo oil supplies to the USA and the EC member-states became a reality.

Irritation with US attitudes and the desire not to be tied down by them was one reason for accepting in London the blunt wording of the Copenhagen declaration. Kissinger's proposal for a coordinated consumer approach to the Arab threat of an oil embargo was rejected by France, which was firmly opposed to any response which would be restricted solely to consumers. The problems were, as France and Britain agreed, at least as much attributable to producers, including the largest producer, the USA.

Table 1. Estimated Outputs per annum of Crude Oil, thousand tons, 1973

USA	495,000
Soviet Union	421,000
Saudi Arabia	412,000
Iran	301,000
Kuwait	112,000
Canada	97,000
Iraq	95,000
Libya	77,000
Algeria	49,000
Qatar	21,700
Egypt	7,500
German Federal Republic	6,638
Austria	2,600

Statistisches Jahrbuch die Bundesrepublik Deutschland (1976)

The decision to use restrictions on oil supply as an incentive to the EC to support Arab pressure for an Israeli withdrawal to the frontiers of Palestine was taken at a meeting in Kuwait on 16 October 1973. As the EC had feared, it was discriminatory. There was to be a five per cent reduction in oil supply to western economies in each month until Israel withdrew and the Palestinians were given the right to self-determination. The Israeli withdrawal was then to be also from East Jerusalem. However, as with the Copenhagen Declaration, so with the skilful resolution of the Arab oil embargo crisis, France and Britain found a basis for cooperation independently from the USA.

If we estimate the total output of crude oil in Western Europe in 1973 at 13,148 tons, of which in the cases of the United Kingdom and France the richest source of supply for refining was from the Middle East, it is easy to see how threatened by an embargo European producers might seem. Of the total oil supply of crude oil to the United Kingdom, between 65 and 70 per cent came from Arab countries. For the Netherlands, threatened with an immediate total embargo, about 58 per cent of crude oil imports came from the Arab world. For the UK the threat seemed to lie in the impact on the balance of payments. A weak trade and payments balance had led to the pound sterling being floated in June 1972, at the very time the European Community was envisaging a unified currency as the first fruits of territorial expansion. Although the UK Treasury department did not think the pound sterling could risk returning to a parity régime, France made it clear that it must do so, otherwise there would be no agreement on multilateral trade and payments systems within the Common Market and no progress towards the European Monetary Union (EMU) which the French government envisaged as a crucial policy for holding the German Federal Republic within the new structure of European integration. The UK's search for political stability in Europe looked as though it might cause domestic economic instability through changes in trade patterns and the breakdown of fixed exchange rates.

The way out of this double trap was made possible, however, by a firmly positive policy towards the Arab oil exporters along the lines Douglas-Home had envisaged, the provision of development aid and technological help, accompanied by supplying weapons. None of this was welcome to or supported by the USA. It was, however, close to the views of the French government under Pompidou.

In 1968 crude petroleum output in the USA made up 3329 million barrels, about 24 per cent of estimated world output. Imports of all oil into the USA amounted in the same year to about 567 million barrels.[13] Of the total value of US imports of crude and partly refined petroleum, 72.3 per cent was imported from other American republics and Canada.[14] While the USA was thus a major importer, much of its supply would be uninterrupted. Imports of crude petroleum into the United Kingdom in the same year attained the highest level they had reached since they began. Oil was the costliest single commodity in the long list of British imports.[15] In value terms, however, UK exports of petroleum and petroleum products amounted to 76.2 per cent of the total import cost of unrefined oil.[16] Furthermore, Britain and France each had worldwide oil reserves, as yet only partially exploited, owned by their international oil companies, particularly in the Middle East.

For western European countries, national output of oil, whether crude or refined, was only one item, and not the most important, in a worldwide pattern of investment in oil resources, crude oil production, and oil refining to produce a wide range of different final products. The same was true for the USA. For western Europe a serious question raised by

---

13 *Statistical Abstract of the United States, 1970*, p. 656, tables 1037 and 1038.
14 *ibid.*, p. 786, table 1229.
15 United Kingdom Central Statistical Office, *Annual Abstract of Statistics*, No. 106, 1969, Table 274.
16 *ibid.*, Table 268.

warfare between Israel and the Arab world was, in the longer run who would control oil in these Middle Eastern fields? The dispute over the nationalisation by the Iranian government of the Anglo-Iranian Oil company in 1951 had shown that the USA, in acting as an intermediary could pave the way to the substitution of British by American control. Cooperation between Western European and American companies was essential in defending the interests of «The West», but competition between them as nations was not to be easily avoided, making it implicit that the member-states of the EC might be wise to seek independently of the USA some common ground in response to the war.

The total Arab oil embargo on the USA would be no more than a gesture, because of the large reserves of oil, national and imported, crude and processed, of which the USA disposed. Restriction of supply to the countries of EEC, only the Netherlands having to cope with a total embargo, would, in contrast, slow down the growth of the Arab economies by severely reducing their export earnings and their level of imports from western Europe. This left open the possibility that the EC would not necessarily stand in line with US plans for a peace agreement. It might, rather, be tempted towards persevering in its insistence that UN Resolution No. 242 should be a fundamental aspect of a peace treaty. To understand the doubts on the Arab side about the reliance which could be placed on the EC states upholding their stated views on the necessity of a return of former Arab territories, we can follow the uncertain path which they took towards bringing peace to the region. Could such a peace be sustained without some degree of Arab catching-up with Israeli technology, especially in armaments? The situation seemed to require an increase in high-technology imports from Europe.

There were some conditions which favoured such an agreement. Oil was, in fact, in oversupply, due to the huge investments and the consequent increase in output made by the major oil producers. The effect on prices was adverse and the competition among sellers was fierce. Middle Eastern countries produced less oil than they would have done in a sellers' market. Middle Eastern governments in some cases put pressure on new companies to speed up production in spite of weak prices. Established oil-producing lands made companies stick to the officially posted prices, although they were unrealistically high.[17] Following the Iranian precedent, in almost every producing state a «National Company» came into being and supported, often by legislative pressure, the policies of the major producers. How the agreement was achieved and what were its successes is recounted in the useful volume by Al-Mani.[18] The common European foreign policy, in this aspect too, was a response to American attitudes towards European integration and to European states which sought closer relations with their Arab oil suppliers as American-Arab relationships deteriorated.

---

17 Stephen Hemsley Longrigg, *Oil in the Middle East. Its Discovery and Development* (3rd edition, Oxford University Press, London, 1968 (under the auspices of the Royal Institute of International Affairs).
18 Saleh A. Al-Mani, *The Euro-Arab Dialogue*, edited by Saleh Al-Shaikhly, New York, St Martin's Press, 1983.

The concept of a Common European policy, of which the Euro-Arab dialogue was a foundation seems to have had less to do with ever-closer sympathies between the Community member-states than with the distaste, and sometimes plain opposition, of Washington for what the Europeans were doing. It hardly needs as explanation an analysis of European anti-Americanism or of American anti-European-integrationism. It had little to do with built in bureaucratic agendas in the European Community, nor from built-in bureaucratic procedures of the European institutions, nor from the institutionalization of the European Community. Its existence was due to more traditional causes of international dissent. It was the outcome of changing points of view in the USA about its role in the post-war period, of a growing economic and diplomatic confidence within «Europe», and of a ready and optimistic purpose by west Europeans and Soviet Russia to secure a peace of long-standing. Whatever threatened that peace was always likely to be countered by a European common policy. A European common foreign policy would always mark the reality that «the West» was far from having a common policy.

Innocents Abroad?
Orientalism and America's New Empire in the Middle East

Douglas Little

In the summer of 1867, Mark Twain, nineteenth-century America's favorite son, steamed east from New York City across the Atlantic and into the Mediterranean, where he would witness one of America's earliest and most memorable encounters with the Muslim world. Accompanying Twain aboard the *S.S. Quaker City* was a band of self-styled American pilgrims whose idealized image of the biblical Holy Land would soon be shattered by the hard realities of the modern Middle East. Twain's account of this odyssey appeared two years later as *The Innocents Abroad,* which quickly became a best-seller. Although published more than a century ago, Twain's comic travelogue provides some intriguing clues about the origins of America's current misadventures in Iraq and elsewhere in the Middle East. Indeed, when read through the lens of fifty years of deepening U.S. involvement in the region, Twain's *Innocents Abroad* becomes a premonition of twentieth-century American cultural imperialism and also helps answer the question that President George W. Bush asked again and again during the dark days after September 11th: «Why do they hate us?»

Because Mark Twain's literary career unfolded against a backdrop of American empire-building during the last half of the nineteenth century, much of what he wrote reads like a critique of expansionist U.S. foreign policies in the age of Grant, McKinley, and Teddy Roosevelt. In 1873, for example, Twain published *The Gilded Age*, an exposé describing the rise of rapacious industrialism and conspicuous consumption in post-Civil War America that foreshadowed the rise of the United States as a truly global power. Twain's two masterworks, *The Adventures of Tom Sawyer* published in 1876 and *The Adventures of Huckleberry Finn* published a decade later, are meditations on the immutable racial hierarchy at the core of the continental empire that white Americans constructed at the expense of people of color. Twain's frequent use of the «N word» has offended many modern readers, but characters like Nigger Jim and Injun Joe are really precursors of the «towel heads» and «camel jockeys» who would become stock figures in American popular culture during the last half of the twentieth century.

The key themes that were implicit in Twain's early work–cultural imperialism, expanding capitalism, and racial hierarchy–became explicit in *To the Person Sitting in Darkness*, the fiery critique of America's «splendid little war» with Spain and its «liberation» of the Philippines that he published in 1901. Outraged by the brutal war that the Roosevelt administration was waging against anti-American insurgents on Luzon and Mindanao at a cost of 4,200 American and 200,000 Filipino lives, Twain saw no evidence that the United States was motivated by innocent altruism or a desire to spread democracy. On the contrary, such altruistic claims were little more than fig leaves designed to conceal a naked quest for a new transoceanic empire in the Pacific. Dismissing claims that America's goals in Asia were very different from those embraced by its European rivals, Twain characterized U.S. policy in the Philippines as imperialism, pure and simple. The way the author of *The Gilded Age* saw it, Wall Street regarded the Pacific archipelago as little more than a set of commercial stepping stones to the China market, which could absorb the excess capacity of American farms and factories. As for Emilio Aguinaldo and the Filipino insurgents whom he led, Washington regarded them as «gooks» who were no more capable of self-government and no more deserving of respect than the blacks and Indians at the bottom of the American hierarchy of race that had deeply disturbed Twain from the very moment he first put pen to paper.

In short, Mark Twain regarded Teddy Roosevelt and other members of the emerging American power elite who advocated empire-building in the Caribbean and the Pacific as bigoted and greedy, not innocent and altruistic. Here's how Twain framed the issue in *To the Person Sitting in Darkness*:

> *Shall we go on conferring our Civilization upon the peoples that sit in darkness, or shall we give those poor things a rest? Shall we bang right ahead in our old-time, loud, pious way, and commit the new century to the game; or shall we sober up and sit down and think it over first?...*
>
> *The Person sitting in Darkness is almost sure to say: 'There is something curious about this—curious and unaccountable. There must be two Americas; one that sets the captive free, and one that takes a once-captive's new freedom away from him, and picks a quarrel with him with nothing to found it on; and then kills him to get his land.'*[1]

When Twain died in 1910, neither he nor other Americans could have imagined that the United States would become an imperial power in the Middle East a century later. Yet the same ingredients that had brought America an empire in the Philippines by 1905–cultural imperialism, economic expansion, and racial hierarchy–would lay the groundwork for a new

---

1 Mark Twain, «To the Person Sitting in Darkness» (February 1901), in Mark Twain, *Collected Tales, Sketches, Speeches, & Essays, 1891–1910* (New York: Library of America, 1992), pp. 457–73. The quotations are at pp. 461, 467.

American empire centered in Iraq by 2005. It is the policies produced by those ingredients, not some innate Islamic hatred of America or Americans, that have sparked the current «jihad» against the United States throughout much of the Muslim world. Let me elaborate.

As I have suggested in my recent book, *American Orientalism*, the story of America's emergence as the major power in the Middle East after 1945 abounds with ironies sufficient to bring a smile to Mark Twain's face. The plot lines revolve around economics, ideology, and race. I will not recount in great detail here today the argument that I have offered there, but I do need to summarize briefly the driving forces behind U.S. policy in the region during the decades after the Second World War. Much of this will come as no surprise to you.

In the beginning, there was oil. When U.S. multinationals first began to pump black gold from the Middle East during the 1930s, it seemed that what was good for Exxon was also good for America, and vice versa. As a result, during the decade after V-J Day a petro-partnership emerged between businessmen and policymakers predicated on keeping Persian Gulf petroleum firmly under U.S. control in order to fuel the economic recovery of America's oil-starved European allies. As late as 1959, the United States remained a net exporter of oil, but fifteen years later rising American consumption and the growing power of the Organization of Petroleum Exporting Countries (OPEC) changed the energy equation, dissolving the petro-partnership and leading Exxon and other multinationals quietly to cast their lots with the producing states. By the 1990s, on average one-third of American petroleum imports came from the Middle East, where U.S. policymakers took great care to cultivate friends in Saudi Arabia and Kuwait while isolating foes in Libya and Iraq. Because neither America's friends and nor its foes were democratically inclined, on the eve of the new millennium most Arabs believed that what mattered most to the United States in the Middle East was oil, not democracy.[2]

From the Arab point of view, the only thing that might have mattered more was Israel. During the half century after Harry Truman made America the first nation to recognize the new Jewish state in May 1948, a «special relationship» evolved between Washington and Tel Aviv, a relationship that generated serious tensions between the United States and the Muslim world.

Critics claimed that the driving force behind the Israeli-American «special relationship» was domestic politics, with bipartisan efforts to woo the «Jewish vote» producing consistently pro-Israel policies.[3] As Peter Hahn has reminded us in his recent book *Caught in the Middle East*, however, there was considerably more to the story than the outcome at the ballot box on the first Tuesday after the first Monday in November. By the mid-1960s, the United States was selling Israel a broad range of military hardware, in part because the Pentagon regarded the Jewish state as a strategic asset against Soviet-backed Arab radicals and in

---

2   Douglas Little, *American Orientalism: The United States and the Middle East since 1945* (Chapel Hill: University of North Carolina Press, 2004), pp. 43–75.
3   *Ibid.*, pp. 77–87.

part because the State Department hoped that providing the Israelis with all manner of conventional weaponry would make them less likely to go nuclear. Much to the chagrin of many Americans and most Arabs, Israel used its newly acquired U.S. tanks and planes to seize the West Bank, Gaza, and the Golan Heights during the 1967 Six Day War and then went nuclear anyway. Four decades later, a quarter-million Israeli settlers have staked claims in the occupied territories, the Israeli arsenal contains a sophisticated array of conventional and unconventional weapons, and most Muslims blame the United States.[4]

America's concerns about Persian Gulf oil and its commitments to Israel were complicated by its Cold War confrontation with Soviet Russia, whose interests in the Middle East were perceived as antithetical to those of the United States. Determined to contain the Kremlin and prevent the spread of communism after 1945, U.S. policymakers expected the United Kingdom to maintain its traditional role as arbiter of Western strategic interests in the region, but nasty clashes with revolutionary nationalists like Iran's Mohammed Mossadegh and Egypt's Gamal Abdel Nasser steadily eroded British influence in the Middle East and eventually forced Britain to withdraw all its troops from the Red Sea to the Persian Gulf in 1971. Eager to prevent Moscow from filling the vacuum, Washington relied increasingly on Muslim partners, first turning to autocrats like the Shah of Iran and later enlisting Islamic radicals like the Afghan mujahadeen to further America's anti-communist aims. According to the logic of containment, «The enemy of my enemy is my friend.» In the short run, such logic kept Iran out of the communist camp and ensnared the Red Army in a bloody quagmire in Afghanistan, but over the long haul, containing the Soviet Union helped put the United States on a collision course with the Ayatollah Khomeini and the Taliban.[5]

As important as oil, Israel, and containment were in shaping U.S. policies in the Middle East after 1945, the most important ingredient was what I have called «American Orientalism,» something far less tangible but far more potent than economic or strategic interests. As the late Edward Said showed in a series of path-breaking books, «orientalism»–the tendency to dismiss Muslims as backward, decadent, and evil–is deeply rooted in the Western psyche. Such stereotypes helped provide a convenient rationale for British and French imperialism in the Middle East throughout the last half of the nineteenth century and the first half of the twentieth. As Mark Twain had predicted as early as 1867, orientalism American-style would play a similar role in the United States.[6]

Stereotypes are dangerous things. Just how dangerous did not become apparent to me until one afternoon in the summer of 1992, when I took my eight-year-old daughter to see the Disney animated classic, *Aladdin*. At one level, the film was all about Aladdin's love for Jasmine, a fable well suited for the pre-teen set. Not very far beneath the surface, however,

---

4   Peter Hahn, *Caught in the Middle East: U.S. Policy Toward the Arab-Israeli Conflict, 1945–1961* (Chapel Hill: University of North Carolina Press, 2004).
5   Little, *American Orientalism*, pp. 117–55.
6   Edward W. Said, *Orientalism* (New York: Pantheon, 1978).

there was an orientalist message straight out of *The Innocents Abroad*. A few minutes after the opening credits rolled, my daughter watched a swarthy Saddam Hussein look-alike croon a song titled «Arabian Nights» whose lyrics went like this:

Oh I come from a land, from a faraway place
Where the caravan camels roam
Where they cut off your ear if the don't like your face
It's barbaric, but hey, it's home

When I asked my daughter afterwards what she thought of *Aladdin*, she said: «I don't know, Dad, do they really cut off your ear if they don't like your face?»

Her response led me to think long and hard about the stereotypes embedded in American popular culture. In a brilliant little volume analyzing perceptions of the Muslim world during the fifty years after 1776, Robert Allison has shown that most Americans familiar with the Crusades, Scheherazade's *1001 One Arabian Nights*, and the Barbary Wars viewed Islam as a despotic, deviant, and dangerous creed whose followers were a mortal threat to the fledgling republic.[7] A century later, popular magazines like *National Geographic* presented the Arabs as an exotic, untrustworthy, and explosive people who bore close watching. Sadly, America's increasing familiarity with the Muslim world after 1945 seems merely to have bred increasing contempt. By the 1990s, *Aladdin* was certainly not unusual in presenting orientalist themes. Anyone watching Arnold Schwartzenegger in *True Lies* or Steven Seagal in *Executive Decision* could quickly see that Hollywood knew who wore white hats and who wore black. Because American policymakers were no less susceptible to such stereotypes than the American public, orientalism helped create powerful mental maps that predisposed the United States to adopt anti-Arab and anti-Muslim attitudes during the last years of the twentieth century and the first years of the twenty-first.[8]

If oil, Israel, containment, and orientalism propelled the United States into the Middle East after 1945, a series of unexpected developments early in the new millennium were critical in the next step–the unprecedented creation of a new American empire in the Middle East. In the aftermath of events of September 11, 2001, President George W. Bush vowed to destroy first Osama bin Laden's al-Qaeda network and then an «Axis of Evil» whose chief member was Iraq's Saddam Hussein. In short order, Bush launched a global war on terror based on an overarching assumption: Islamic radicals hate Americans for who they are, not for what they do. Heavily influenced by «orientalist» Middle East experts both inside and outside the U.S. government, the Bush administration has refused for nearly four years to reconsider key American policies in the region and has instead reiterated the need to fight

---

7   Robert J. Allison, *The Crescent Obscured: The United States and the Muslim World, 1776–1815* (New York: Oxford University Press, 1995).
8   Little, *American Orientalism*, pp. 17–42, 326–27.

fire with fire. One principal result has been a political and military conflagration in Baghdad which shows no sign of burning itself out any time soon.

A quick look at Bush's approach to the Middle East confirms that the old ingredients that shaped America's relations with the region still matter. Take oil. Four months before September 11th, Vice President Dick Cheney handed his boss a report on America's energy future whose basic assumption was that «Middle East oil producers will remain central to world oil security» and whose principal conclusion was that American interests would be best served by forcing OPEC members like Saudi Arabia and Iraq «to open up areas of their energy sectors to foreign investment» by U.S. multinationals.[9] Although few would go as far as journals like *Mother Jones*, which claimed that the primary goal of the American invasion of Iraq in March 2003 was to gain control of Saddam Hussein's petroleum reserves, many believe that rising oil prices and dwindling domestic supplies led the oil man in the Oval Office to see a big economic bonus for Washington's military assault on Baghdad.[10] After U.S. troops showed less interest in safeguarding Iraq's classical antiquities than in protecting its oil refineries, however, and after Halliburton, Cheney's old firm, was awarded half a billion dollars to rebuild Iraq's oil infrastructure, critics of the American invasion could be forgiven for discounting Secretary of Defense Donald Rumsfeld's strident prewar disclaimer that the Bush administration's showdown with Saddam had «nothing to do with oil, literally nothing to do with oil.»[11]

Like oil, the special relationship with Israel has remained a central feature of American policy in the Middle East during the Bush era. In 2004, Israel received over $3 billion in U.S. economic and military aid, more than any other nation. Tel Aviv's clout in Washington remains stronger and more bipartisan than ever, with Democrats determined to strengthen their historic ties to Jewish voters and with Republicans eager to deepen their connections with right-wing pro-Israel Christian evangelicals. Since September 11th, public support for Israel has risen steadily in the United States, where the average American has drawn parallels between Palestinian suicide bombers in Jerusalem and Osama bin Laden's murderous attacks on New York City and Washington, D.C. The Israeli public has returned the favor, making George W. Bush more popular in the Jewish state than any occupant of the White House in four decades.[12]

Nevertheless, America's relations with Israel have been strained during the past four years because of disagreements over how best to resolve the Israeli-Palestinian conflict. Although Bush's refusal throughout his first term to meet with Yasser Arafat signaled mounting White House frustration with the upsurge of Palestinian terror after 2001, the Texas Republican

9   National Energy Policy Development Group, *Reliable, Affordable, and Environmentally Sound Energy for America's Future* (May 2001), x, 8.1–8.13.
10 Robert Dreyfuss, «The Thirty-Year Itch,» *Mother Jones* (March/April 2003).
11 Rumsfeld and Chalabi quoted in Michael Renner, «Post-Saddam Iraq: Linchpin of a New Oil Order,» *Foreign Policy In Focus* (Jan. 2003): 5, http://www.foreignpolicy-infocus.org.
12 *New York Times*, 3 May 2002, A10, and 13 May 2002, A8.

was also frequently at odds with Israeli Prime Minister Ariel Sharon, whose plans to expand Jewish settlements on the West Bank made prospects for peace ever more remote. Hoping that the swift American victory over Saddam Hussein's Iraq in April 2003 would encourage the two sides to stop shooting and start talking, one month later Bush unveiled a «road map to peace» calling for Arafat to halt terrorism against Israel and for Sharon to freeze settlements in the occupied territories as the first steps toward a two-state solution. Even the best road map is useless, of course, unless those driving along the highway pay attention to the road signs. For two years, Ariel Sharon showed little interest in following American directions. Although President Bush applauded Sharon during an Oval Office meeting in April 2005 for taking steps to remove Israeli settlers from Gaza, he also reminded him that «Israel has obligations under the road map... [which] clearly says no expansion of settlements.» When Prime Minister Sharon retorted that the existing settlements on the West Bank would continue to grow and that the major population centers «will remain in Israel's hands under any future final status agreement,» his host tried to make the best out of a bad situation by telling reporters that «new realities on the ground» made it «unrealistic» to expect the Israelis to remove all of their settlements from all of the occupied territories.[13]

If oil and Israel have remained constant factors in shaping American policy in the Middle East during the past fifteen years, the collapse of the Soviet Union and the end of the Cold War after 1989 have meant that the containment of Moscow was no longer a central feature of Washington's military and diplomatic strategy in the region. Yet as the Clinton administration struggled during the 1990s to bring order to a chaotic post-Cold War world wracked by ethnic and religious conflict, some American observers began to argue that a «green threat»–radical Islam–was supplanting the earlier «red threat»–international communism–that had kept every American president from Harry Truman to Ronald Reagan awake at night. By the time that George W. Bush took office in January 2001, containing Islamic extremism was as important for U.S. policymakers as containing Soviet subversion had been a generation earlier.

As early as 1990, Bernard Lewis, a Princeton historian and founding father of the field of Middle Eastern Studies, was predicting a «clash of civilizations» between Islam and America that would make the ideological rivalry between Moscow and Washington seem tame by comparison. In an article entitled the «Roots of Muslim Rage» published in the *Atlantic Monthly* on the eve of Saddam Hussein's stunning invasion of Kuwait, Lewis contended that the recent upsurge of «intense–and violent–[Islamic] resentment of the West» was actually the result of «a long series of attacks and counterattacks, jihads and crusades, conquests and reconquests» that had produced knee-jerk Muslim hatred of the infidels. Nevertheless, President George H. W. Bush, «Number Forty-One,» proved unwilling to transform the First Gulf War into a crusade and stopped short of deposing the Iraqi dictator in early 1991. By

---

13 *New York Times*, 12 April 2005, A1.

the time that Bill Clinton moved into the Oval Office two years later, Middle East watchers like Harvard political scientist Samuel P. Huntington worried that the new administration, like its predecessor, would pay too much attention to economic globalization and too little to Islamic fundamentalism. Inspired by the writings of Bernard Lewis and funded by the neo-conservative Olin Foundation, Huntington wrote a widely-read article in the summer of 1993 for *Foreign Affairs* entitled «The Clash of Civilizations» which in effect called for the «containment» of the Muslim threat. Although critics charged him with «Islamophobia,» Huntington insisted that on the eve of the new millennium, culture mattered more than economics or ideology. «Faith and family, blood and belief, are what people identify with and what they will fight and die for,» he concluded the following winter. «And that is why the clash of civilizations is replacing the Cold War as the central phenomenon of global politics.»[14]

Preoccupied with brokering an Israeli-Palestinian peace agreement and halting the brutal ethnic strife in the Balkans, where Serbian nationalists claimed that only by «cleansing» Yugoslavia of its Muslim minority could Christendom prevent the triumph of radical Islam, President Clinton and his top advisers believed that embracing Huntington's oversimplified view of the world would merely make bad situations worse. The Cold War was over, the Arkansas Democrat was fond of saying, and Americans needed to realize that the emerging global system was multipolar, not bipolar. National Security Adviser Anthony Lake explicitly took issue with Huntington's approach in a well publicized speech in the spring of 1994. «Some theorists have suggested that there is no common ground for understanding between the West and the rest–only the prospect of confrontation and conflict. They assert that the United States, as the sole remaining superpower, should lead a new crusade against Islam,» Lake told the Washington Institute for Near East Policy on 17 May. «In the quest for a new ideology to rally against, they believe fundamentalism would replace communism as the West's designated theat.» Lake had just five words for Samuel Huntington: «The Clinton administration strongly disagrees.»[15] James Woolsey, Clinton's CIA director, echoed Lake's remarks four months later. «We should not accept the notion that the 'Red Menace' that dominated our lives for nearly half a century is now being replaced by a 'Green Menace' sweeping through the Arab world,» Woolsey warned in September 1994. «The time of the Great Crusades belongs in the Middle Ages, not as we prepare to usher in the 21st century.»[16]

---

14   Samuel P. Huntington, «The Clash of Civilizations?» *Foreign Affairs*, 72 (Summer 1993): 22–49, and «If Not Civilizations, What? Paradigms of the Post-Cold War World,» *Foreign Affairs*, 72 (November/December 1993): 194. On the roots of Huntington's world view, see Robert D. Kaplan, «Looking the World in the Eye,» *Atlantic Monthly* (Dec. 2001): 68–82.
15   Anthony Lake, «Conceptualizing U.S. Strategy in the Middle East,» delivered at the Washington Institute for Near East Policy, 17 May 1994, *www.washingtoninstitute.org*.
16   R. James Woolsey, «Challenges to Peace in the Middle East,» delivered at the Wye Plantation Policy Conference, 23 Sept. 1994, *www.washingtoninstitute.org*.

Huntington begged to differ. In a book-length rebuttal that appeared two years later, he did not mince words. «Wherever one looks, along the perimeter of Islam, Muslims have problems living peaceably with their neighbors,» Huntington pointed out with an eye to recent strife from Southeast Europe to Central Asia. «In the early 1990s Muslims were engaged in more intergroup violence than were non-Muslims, and two-thirds to three-quarters of inter-civilizational wars were between Muslims and non-Muslims,» he concluded. «Islam's borders *are* bloody, and so are its innards.»[17] By the end of the decade, neo-conservative academics like Daniel Pipes were calling radical Islam the last and most dangerous of the totalitarian ideologies spawned during the twentieth century and were accusing the Clinton administration of «appeasement» for negotiating with Arab radicals like Yasser Arafat.[18]

As far as «Number Forty-Three,» George W. Bush, was concerned, the catastrophic attacks of September 11th merely confirmed just how accurate Lewis, Huntington, and Pipes were. Bush the Younger's gut reaction was to call for a «crusade» against Osama bin Laden and the Taliban, the Islamic radicals who made Al Qaeda welcome in Afghanistan. Deputy Secretary of Defense Paul Wolfowitz, a leading neo-conservative who counted Lewis and Huntington among his friends, framed the Bush administration's new global war on terror the same way that George Kennan and other advocates of anti-communist containment had framed the Cold War struggle against the Soviet Union during the late 1940s. «From the beginning of the war on terrorism, we have stressed the importance of understanding the nature of our enemy as a network. Al-Qaeda is not a snake that can be killed by lopping off its head. It is more analogous to a disease that has infected many parts of a healthy body,» Wolfowitz told a congressional committee in June 2002. «Our intention... [is] not only to deprive the terrorists of a sanctuary in Afghanistan where they could safely plan, train, and organize, but also to capture and kill terrorists, and to drain the swamp in which they breed.»[19]

As the Islamic «green threat» supplanted the communist «red threat» in the minds of America's national security managers, all the old orientalist stereotypes so central to earlier U.S. policies in the Middle East resurfaced. During the days immediately after September 11th, Bush himself cautioned Americans not to tar all Muslims with the brush of terrorism, but the west Texas born-again Christian rhetoric that he employed to mobilize the country against Osama bin Laden sounded a lot like old-fashioned orientalism to some ears. Likewise, the racial profiling of Arabs at airports and elsewhere and the aggressive surveillance of

---

17   Samuel P. Huntington, *The Clash of Civilizations and the Remaking of World Order* (New York, 1996), pp. 256–58.
18   Daniel Pipes, «There Are No Moderates: Dealing with Fundamentalist Islam,» *The National Interest*, No. 41 (Fall 1995), pp. 48–57. For an updated account of this article including the events of the late 1990s, see Daniel Pipes, *Militant Islam Reaches America* (New York, 2002), pp. 38–51.
19   Wolfowitz testimony, 26 June 2002, in U.S. Congress, Senate, Committee on Foreign Relations, *Afghanistan: Building Stability, Avoiding Chaos*, (Washington, DC: GPO, 2002), available on-line at *http://www.access.gpo.gov/congress/senate*.

Muslim groups across the country by the newly created Office of Homeland Security raised public fears of internal subversion to levels unmatched since the 1950s. Daniel Pipes, for example, reminded his readers that the McCarren-Walter Act, a vestige of the anti-communist hysteria of the McCarthy era, was still on the books and could be used to justify the internment of Muslim Americans during a national emergency. The capture of John Walker Lindh, a California convert to Islam who fought alongside the Taliban against GI's in Afghanistan, confirmed for many Americans that the Muslim menace at home was more serious than they had suspected.[20]

Nowhere was this orientalist outlook more deeply embedded than the American military, the men and women at the front lines of the global war on terror from Kabul to Baghdad. In the heat of battle, it is easy to demonize the enemy, especially in a place like Iraq, where by the fall of 2003 the Pentagon's undersized expeditionary force of 150,000 troops confronted a ruthless anti-American insurgency. The string of car bombs, ambushes, and kidnappings that paralyzed the Iraqi capital left Americans both abroad and at home with frayed nerves and short tempers. Asked by a reporter how things were going in October 2003, one GI manning a checkpoint in Baghdad offered this blistering assessment of the Iraqi national character. «If you really want to know,» he told the *New York Times*, «I'm sick of being in a country where lying is the national pastime.»[21] With American casualties mounting in Baghdad, syndicated radio talk show host Dr. Laura Schlesinger chastised a caller from Baltimore one month later for allowing her daughter to visit a local mosque as part of a program to foster intercultural understanding. «I am horrified that you would let her go,» Schlesinger snapped. «I am so sick and tired of all the Arab-American groups whining and complaining about some kind of treatment. What culture and what religion were all the murderers of 9/11? They murdered us. That's the culture you want your daughter to learn about?»[22]

Lieutenant General Jerry Boykin, whom Secretary of Defense Donald Rumsfeld had tapped to lead the Pentagon's new top-secret counter-terrorist unit, was even blunter. A veteran of the U.S. Army Special Forces with combat experience against Muslim guerrillas in Somalia, Boykin cast the war in Iraq in religious terms. In a series of prayer breakfasts and right-wing pep talks during 2003, Boykin insisted that America's greatest foe was not Osama bin Laden or Saddam Hussein but rather Islam itself. «The enemy is none of these people I have showed you here,» he told a Florida audience after one of his inspirational slide shows. «The enemy is a spiritual enemy. He's called the principality of darkness. The enemy is a guy called Satan.» Islamic radicals had targeted the United States not because they were unhappy with U.S. policies but simply because they hated Americans. «They're after us because we're a Christian nation,» Boykin concluded. Calling for what amounted to a new crusade against

20 Pipes, *Militant Islam Reaches America*, pp. xvi, 141–42.
21 «Baffled Occupiers, or the Missed Understandings,» *New York Times*, 22 Oct. 2003.
22 Schlesinger comments, 17 Nov. 2003, www.drlaura.com/listen.

an old infidel, Boykin recalled with pride what he had told a captured Somali guerrilla leader in Mogadishu a decade earlier: «Well, you know what I knew, that my God was bigger than his. I knew that my God was a real God, and his was an idol.»[23]

Americans eager to understand what motivated Islamic zealots like Osama bin Laden frequently turned to Middle East «experts» whose views, when stripped of their academic jargon, were at bottom not much different from Boykin's. One such expert was Raphael Patai, who taught cultural anthropology at Columbia University and whose best seller, *The Arab Mind*, became a handbook for American readers seeking to determine what ailed the Middle East during the 1970s. Patai contended that faulty toilet training, prolonged breast feeding, and frequent bullying produced an extraordinary propensity for interpersonal violence and sexual aggression among young Arab men, who were obsessed with having sex and making war. Almost three decades after *The Arab Mind* first appeared, Patai's publisher brought out a new edition in the wake of September 11th that quickly became a must read at the Pentagon as the Bush administration prepared for war with Iraq in early 2003. Colonel Norvell De Atkine, a West Point graduate who served for eight years as a military attaché in Lebanon, Jordan, and Egypt before accepting a teaching post at the John F. Kennedy Special Warfare School at Fort Bragg, North Carolina, set the tone in the foreword to the 2002 edition: «At the institution where I teach military officers, *The Arab Mind* forms the basis of my cultural instruction.»[24] Arabs were prisoners of religious stultification and tribalism, De Atkine added, which trapped them in «a pervasive cultural and political environment that stifles development of initiative, independent thinking, and innovation.»[25] When Seymour Hersh, the dean of American investigative journalists, interviewed U.S. military officials about torture at Abu Ghraib prison a year later, many confirmed that the army's use of sexual humiliation as a technique to «break» Iraqi prisoners was based on a careful reading of *The Arab Mind*. Indeed, one unnamed academic told Hersh that by the time that the first bunker-busting bombs fell on Baghdad in March 2003, Patai's book had become «the bible of the neocons on Arab behavior» because it confirmed «one, that Arabs understand only force and, two, that the biggest weakness of Arabs is shame and humiliation.»[26] Although critics charged that Hersh had exaggerated the importance of *The Arab Mind*, by 2004 it was required reading both for the Coalition Provisional Authority's «Operation Iraq Freedom Seminar» in Baghdad and for the U.S. Army's counterinsurgency course at Fort Carson, Colorado.[27]

---

23 Lisa Myers, «Top Terrorist Hunter's Divisive Views,» *MSNBC.COM*, 15 Oct, 2003.
24 Lee Smith, «Inside the American Mind,» *Slate*, 27 May 2004; Brian Whitaker, «The Arab Mind in Neoconservative Ideology and Military Doctrine,» *Guardian*, 24 May 2004.
25 Norvell De Atkine, «Foreword,» in Raphael Patai, *The Arab Mind* (Hatherleigh Press, 2002).
26 Seymour Hersh, «The Gray Zone,» *New Yorker*, 24 May 2004, p. 42.
27 Captain Charles Kyle, «Operation Iraqi Freedom Seminar–Read Ahead,» May 2004, *www.chuckkyle.com/EWA*; Colonel H. R. McMaster, «Brave Rifles Reading List for Operation Iraqi Freedom,» 1 Nov. 2004, *www.carson.army.mil/UNITS/3RD%20ACR*.

Despite what Hersh's sources told him about Patai, however, the most influential academic expert on the Middle East in George W. Bush's Washington remained Princeton's Bernard Lewis. Four months after September 11th, the *Atlantic Monthly* published «What Went Wrong?», Lewis's elegant account of how «Muslim civilization, once a mighty enterprise, has fallen low.» Eschewing Patai's use of popular psychology, Lewis took aim at Arab autocrats like Saddam Hussein. «For the oppressive but ineffectual governments that rule much of the Middle East, finding targets to blame serves a useful, indeed an essential, purpose–to explain the poverty that they have failed to alleviate and to justify the tyranny that they have introduced,» Lewis concluded. «They seek to deflect the mounting anger of their unhappy subjects toward other, outside targets.» In short, Lewis's answer to the question «Why do they hate us?» was: «It's not us, it's them.»[28]

Among those inside Bush's inner circle most intrigued by Lewis's writings was Vice President Dick Cheney, who by late 2002 was emerging as the leading war hawk in Number Forty-Three's administration. Looking for a pretext for toppling Saddam Hussein, Cheney made Lewis his frequent dinner partner in the months preceding Operation Iraqi Freedom. The Princeton historian obliged by providing an ingenious rationale for regime change in Iraq based on what had occurred eighty years earlier in Turkey, where Kemal Ataturk, a secular modernizer, had launched a «revolution from above» designed to westernize his country politically and economically while preserving its Turkish identity. In Ataturk's Turkey, Islam had become the odd man out. If the United States was to find an antidote to radical Islam, it must identify the Arab equivalent of Kemal Ataturk, someone capable of bringing the Arabs into the modern world. «The Islamic world is now at the beginning of the 15th century,» Lewis told a reporter after Saddam's fall, while «the Western world is at the beginning of the 21st century.» Convinced that the Muslim world was «on the verge of its Reformation» that would at long last produce the separation of church and state, Lewis favored exporting democracy at gunpoint to places like Iraq, where the American-led Coalition Provisional Authority propped up secular pro-Western figures like Ahmad Chalabi and Ayad Allawi.[29]

Top State Department officials, however, argued that the American quest for an Arab Ataturk was more likely to succeed if Washington relied more on public relations and diplomacy and less on political manipulation and military force. As a first step, Secretary of State Colin Powell established the Middle East Peace Initiative, which focused on innovative «people-to-people» programs designed to humanize Americans in Muslim eyes. Then in early 2003, Powell persuaded the White House to set up an «Advisory Group on Public Diplomacy in the Arab and Muslim World» headed by Edward Djerejian, who had served as Assistant Secretary of State for Middle East a decade earlier during the administration of George H.W. Bush.

---

28 Bernard Lewis, «What Went Wrong?» *Atlantic Monthly* (Jan. 2002), p. 45.
29 Michael Hersh, «Misreading Islam,» *Washington Monthly*, 12 Nov. 2004.

Djerejian and his team spent three months reviewing surveys of Arab public opinion and shuttling from Cairo and Damascus to Dakar, Rabat, and other Muslim capitals to determine the political temperature of the region before returning to Washington. On October 1, Djerejian released an eighty-page report, *Changing Minds, Winning Peace*, which concluded bluntly that «hostility toward America has reached shocking levels» in the Muslim world. The report's principal findings did not make for pleasant reading at the Bush White House. For example, Djerejian's team confirmed that «shortly before the war against Saddam Hussein, by a greater than two-to-one margin, Muslims surveyed in Saudi Arabia, Qatar, and Jordan said the United States was a more serious threat than Iraq.» Al-Arabiyya and other satellite television stations were broadcasting documentaries like «The Americanization of Islam,» whose story line «was that the United States had embarked on a sinister plot to change the 1,500-year-old religion.» Throughout the Muslim world, the men and women whom Djerejian's task force encountered were «genuinely distressed at the plight of the Palestinians and at the role they perceived the United States to be playing, and they are genuinely distressed by the situation in Iraq.» In not so many words, Djerejian and his colleagues seemed to be saying that, with all due respect to Bernard Lewis, «they hate us because of our policies, *not* because of who we are.»[30]

The Advisory Group on Public Diplomacy may have gotten the diagnosis right, but the jury is still out regarding their prescription. Although the Djerejian task force admitted that «sugar-coating and fast talking are no solutions,» they nevertheless recommended a multi-million dollar public diplomacy campaign that seemed at times both sweet and glib. After seizing control of the Iraqi radio and television system following the fall of Saddam Hussein, the State Department approved a «Shared Values» media blitz emphasizing how Muslims benefitted from religious toleration in America and created a glossy youth-oriented magazine called «Hi» that profiled Arab-American celebrities like Tony Shaloub. Neither of these initiatives, however, played well with Iraqi audiences, who dismissed them as Madison Avenue spin designed to distract attention from the American-led occupation of Baghdad.[31] When White House ideologues launched a public relations offensive later that year to sell the Arab world on Bush's «open market» approach to economic development, they were inadvertently betrayed by incompetent linguists, whose oxymoronic translation of concepts like «privatization» as «castration» and «multilateralism» as «polygamy» evoked bawdy laughter from Baghdad to Beirut.[32]

I myself learned just how difficult it could be to sell America's virtues to the Muslim world a year and a half ago when I was invited to speak to twenty-five Arab college students

---

30 Report of the Advisory Group on Public Diplomacy for the Arab and Muslim World, *Changing Minds, Winning Peace*, 1 Oct. 2003, *http://www.state.gov/documents*.
31 Michael Holtzman, «Washington's Sour Sales Pitch,» *New York Times*, 4 Oct. 2003.
32 Yvonne Haddad, «Islam in the Mind of America,» presented at the Annual Conference of the German Association of American Studies, 4 June 2004, University of Mannheim, Mannheim, Germany.

who had spent their summer at Dickinson College under the auspices of the State Department's Middle East Peace Initiative taking crash courses on U.S. government and history and sampling the American way of life. Although my listeners were much impressed by the two days that they spent shopping in New York City and touring the Smithsonian in Washington D.C, a few minutes into my critique of Bush's Middle East policies they lambasted me as an apologist for American imperialism, castigated the United States for pursuing pro-Israel policies, and insisted that the attacks of September 11th were the result of a CIA-Mossad plot. After I finished speaking, several of the students came up to me to say, in effect, «We hope you understand that we don't hate you, but we do hate your country's policies.»

What seemed to anger those Arab students more even than the Pentagon's «shock and awe» military tactics in Iraq was the Bush administration's plans to build nations and export democracy throughout the region, a scheme that reeked of hypocrisy. My listeners had not failed to notice, for example, that the Edward Djerejian who sought to change minds and win hearts by marketing the American democratic tradition through the Arab media in 2003 was the same man who, a decade earlier, had rationalized an Algerian military crackdown that prevented Islamic radicals from winning free elections with the words: «While we believe in the principle of 'one person, one vote,' we do not support 'one person, one vote, one time.'» In simple English, Djerejian was implying that Islam was antithetical to democracy.[33] What applied to Algeria in 1992 seemed also to apply in post-Saddam Iraq. Richard Haass, one of Secretary of State Colin Powell's closest advisers, had made it clear long before the first U.S. tank rolled into Baghdad that building a democratic system there would take time. «No one should confuse promoting democracy with holding parliamentary elections the next day–in which case the Islamists would do well,» he explained in November 2002. In the Muslim world, Haass continued, political change needed to be introduced carefully, from the top down. «Supporting an authoritarian leader who is a modernizer and is willing to gradually loosen the reins,» Haass concluded in words that echoed Bernard Lewis, «that essentially should be our policy.»[34]

More senior members of the Bush team were somewhat more circumspect in describing what many critics saw as American empire-building in the Middle East. Paul Wolfowitz, for example, was among the first to admit that «Iraq isn't ready for Jeffersonian democracy.» Yet he remained a relentless supporter of regime change in Baghdad because of what it might mean for the entire region. «I think if it's significant for Iraq, it's going to cast a very large shadow,» Wolfowitz predicted in September 2002, «starting with Syria and Iran, but across the whole Arab world, I think.»[35] Condoleeza Rice, Bush's national security adviser, placed

33 Edward Djerejian, «The US and the Middle East in a Changing World,» 8 June 1992, «U.S. State Department Electronic Research Collection,» *http://dosfan.lib.edu/ERC.*
34 Haass quoted in Nicholas Lemann, «Order of Battle,» *New Yorker,* (18 Nov. 2002), 46.
35 Wolfowitz quoted in Bill Keller, «The Sunshine Warrior,» *New York Times Magazine* (22 Sept. 2002), 51.

this argument into a more general framework. «We do not seek to impose democracy on others,» she told the Council on Foreign Relations on 1 October 2002. «Our vision of the future is not one where every person eats Big Macs and drinks Coke–or where every nation has a bicameral legislature with 535 members.» Insisting that the Bush administration wished only «to help create conditions in which people can claim a freer future for themselves,» Rice looked forward «to one day standing for these aspirations in a free and unified Iraq.»[36]

That day arrived sooner than many Americans expected, because the president whom Condoleeza Rice served chose to throw caution to the wind by rejecting the time-honored doctrine of containment that had guided every U.S. administration for the preceding fifty years in favor of a radically different policy based on preventive war. The new national security strategy that Bush unveiled in October 2002 endorsed the principle that the best defense is a good offense. The president elaborated on this rationale three months later in his annual State of the Union address. «After Sept. 11, the doctrine of containment just doesn't hold any water, as far as I'm concerned,» Bush told a national television audience on January 31, 2003. «I told you the strategic vision of our country shifted dramatically, and it shifted dramatically because we now recognize that oceans no longer protect us, that we're vulnerable to attack.» Bush's embrace of the doctrine of preventive war marked the culmination of six years of brainstorming among neo-conservatives like Dick Cheney, Paul Wolfowitz, and Donald Rumsfeld, all three of whom were founding members of the Project for a New American Century, a right-wing think tank whose overarching goal was to make the United States the world's only legitimate military superpower.[37]

In March 2003, Thomas Barnett, a key member of Rumsfeld's brains trust, published a much-discussed article in *Esquire* entitled «The Pentagon's New Map» spelling out the Bush administration's brief for toppling Saddam Hussein. Confessing that war with Iraq was «not only necessary and inevitable, but also good,» Barnett argued that «the only thing that will change that nasty environment and open the floodgates for change is if some external power steps in and plays Leviathan full-time.» Terming Iraq «the Yugoslavia of the Middle East,» he predicted that «as baby sitting jobs go, this one will be a doozy, making our lengthy efforts in postwar Germany and Japan look simple in retrospect.»[38] A year later, Barnett expanded these ideas into a best-selling book that offered an even blunter prognosis. «It is not enough for the Bush administration to say that our new strategic focus is an 'arc of instability' that stretches across the Muslim-dominated regions of North Africa, the Persian Gulf, Central Asia, and Southeast Asia,» Barnett insisted. «America needs to understand the larger global conflict we join when we seek to transform Iraq from 'rogue regime' to model Arab democracy. It is an enduring conflict between those who want to see disconnected societies like Sad-

---

36   Rice remarks, 1 Oct. 2002, http://www.whitehouse.gov/news.
37   James Mann, *Rise of the Vulcans: The History of Bush's War Cabinet* (New York: Viking, 2004), pp. 238, 243.
38   Thomas P. M. Barnett, «The Pentagon's New Map,» *Esquire* (March 2003).

dam's Iraq join the global community defined by globalization's Functioning Core and others who will do whatever it takes in terms of violence to prevent these societies from being–in their minds–assimilated into a 'sacrilegious global economic empire' lorded over by the United States.»[39]

Washington's chief babysitter among the rogues in Iraq would be L. Paul Bremer, whom President Bush named as head of the Coalition Provisional Authority and de facto American proconsul in Baghdad in May 2003. In short order, Bremer disbanded both the Iraqi army and the Iraqi provisional government and made no secret that he believed that the Iraqi people were simply not ready for democracy. Although his actions helped spark a bloody insurgency that has cost thousands of Iraqi lives during the past two years, Bremer has never wavered in his belief that the American occupation of Iraq was absolutely necessary to ensure the country's liberation. «Being an occupying power is not a comfortable thing for most Americans to comprehend, and it certainly is the case that when you are an occupying power you have not only responsibilities but, as you exercise those responsibilities, you're going to have friction,» he told an American reporter in August 2003. «It happens. More people get killed in New York every night than get killed in Baghdad. The fact of life is that here will never be such a thing as one hundred per cent security–it doesn't exist.»[40]

During a visit to Clark University in April 2005, however, Bremer insisted that regime change on the banks of the Euphrates had already made the United States more secure by extirpating the roots of terrorism and preventing Osama bin Laden from making Baghdad the capital of a «global anti-American Islamic caliphate.» I asked him point blank whether he or his colleagues had made any major mistakes in Iraq. He replied «absolutely not» and asked me whether I had read *An End to Evil*, the new book written by two of the Bush administration's favorite neo-conservatives, Richard Perle and David Frum. When I said that I had not, he paraphrased their chief argument for me as follows: America has a responsibility to export democracy to the Muslim world, whether Arab radicals and Islamic militants like it or not. I replied that this sounded an awful lot like old-fashioned orientalism to me. A quick look at Frum and Perle's book confirms that they regard militant Islam is the driving force behind a new «axis of evil» whose ideas, like those promoted earlier by fascism and communism, are antithetical to everything that the United States holds dear. If America is to win this «war of ideas,» Frum and Perle believe that Americans must become more comfortable with the idea of war. «Nobody thinks that it will be fast or easy to bring democracy to the Middle East,» they conclude. «Much more often than not, democracy will not have a chance unless it is aided from outside–and by force, if necessary.»[41]

---

39 Thomas P. M. Barnett, *The Pentagon's New Map: War and Peace in the Twenty-First Century* (New York: G. P. Putnam's Sons, 2004), p. 43.
40 Bremer quoted in Jon Lee Anderson, «Letter from Iraq: Out on the Street,» *New Yorker* (15 Nov. 2004), 74.
41 David Frum and Richard Perle, *An End to Evil: How to Win the War on Terror* (New York, 2003), pp. 160, 278.

Two Middle Easterners, one Arab and the other Israeli, were also high on the Bush administration's reading list because they echoed Frum and Perle's views. Fouad Ajami, a Lebanese-born specialist in Arab nationalism and long-time colleague of Paul Wolfowitz at Johns Hopkins University, emerged as an increasingly strident advocate of American intervention in the Middle East in the wake of the 1991 Gulf War. By early 2003, Ajami was a frequent guest on national network television, where he offered such strong support for toppling Saddam Hussein that *The Nation* magazine labelled him «a native informant.»[42] In a May 2005 *Wall Street Journal* opinion piece entitled «Bush Country,» Ajami insisted that despite the deepening insurgency in Iraq, the democratic was spreading throughout the region because «a conservative American president had come bearing the gift of Wilsonian redemption.»[43] Even more influential was Natan Sharansky, a Soviet dissident-turned-Israeli politician, whose new book, *The Case for Democracy*, was one of the inspirations for George W. Bush's second inaugural address. «The case against democracy in the Middle East appears compelling,» Sharansky confessed. «There has *never* been an Arab democracy, and with the exception of a handful of tyrannies around the world, the world's most repressive regimes are in the Middle East.» With firm leadership from the United States, however, he was convinced that if given the choice, even Arabs would «prefer a *free* society to a *fear* society.»[44] President Bush could not have agreed more and invited Sharansky to the White House to discuss the book one week after November 2004 elections. After endorsing the Israeli's ideas on the steps of the U.S. Capitol on 20 January 2005, Number Forty-Three removed any remaining doubts about where he stood on the matter. «I felt like his book just confirmed what I believe,» Bush told reporters at the end of the month. «That thinking, that's part of my presidential DNA.»[45]

There were fresh indications during early 2005 that other Americans shared Bush's orientalist DNA. A few days before the second inaugural, for example, the Fox television network, whose news division was already renowned for its hard-edged «take-no-prisoners» approach to the Muslim world, launched the fourth season of its highly rated action series «24» with a story line featuring Kiefer Sutherland battling a Muslim «fifth column» inside America. After a wake-up signal from al-Qaeda, Islamic sleeper cells in quick succession kidnap the Secretary of Defense, murder innocent school girls, and attempt to convert America's nuclear power plants into weapons of mass destruction. When the Council on American-Islamic Relations (CAIR) filed an anti-discrimination complaint with the Federal Communications Commission, Fox agreed to run public service announcements urging viewers not to assume that the only good Muslim was a dead one. Meanwhile, Sutherland managed to

---

42   Adam Shatz, «The Native Informant,» *The Nation*, 28 April 2003.
43   Fouad Ajami, «Bush Country,» *Wall Street Journal*, 16 May 2005.
44   Natan Sharansky, with Ron Dermer, *The Case for Democracy: The Power of Freedom to Overcome Tyranny and Terror* (New York: Public Affairs Press, 2004), pp. 37–38.
45   Elisabeth Bumiller, «Bush's Book Club Picks a New Favorite,» *New York Times*, 31 Jan. 2005.

escape several harrowing brushes with death at the hands of Muslim fanatics before triumphing over evil, right on schedule, during the Nielsen «sweeps week» in May.[46] Columnist Ann Coulter, the darling of the neo-conservatives whom *Time* magazine labeled «Ms. Right» in an April 25th cover story, was even blunter than Fox. Speaking at a reception for the Conservative Political Action Conference (CPAC) in February 2005, the blonde, mini-skirted, and sharp-tongued pundit ridiculed CAIR's allegations that American intelligence agencies employed torture against suspected Islamic terrorists in the United States. «It's completely insane stuff. 'The government flew me to Las Vegas and made me have sex with a horse,'» she told her friends in CPAC, adding: «Liberals are about to become the last people to figure out that Arabs lie.»[47] In light of revelations of the brutal actions of U.S. military and intelligence officials at Abu Ghraib and Guantanamo Bay during 2004, both liberals and Arabs could be forgiven for suggesting that Ann Coulter was the one who was completely insane.

One way to measure the chasm separating America from the Muslim world in 2005 might be to imagine a conversation between Ann Coulter and Osama bin Laden. A better way, however, would be to examine the words of two poets, one American and one Arab. One year after the September 11th attacks, Billy Collins, the poet laureate of the United States, went to Ground Zero in New York City to read his heartbreaking poem «The Names,» a meditation on what Americans lost on that awful day.[48] Let me read you part of his poem:

> *Yesterday, I lay awake in the palm of the night.*
> *A fine rain stole in, unhelped by any breeze,*
> *And when I saw the silver glaze in the windows,*
> *I started with A, with Ackerman, as it happened,*
> *Then Baxter and Calabro,*
> *Davis and Eberling, names falling into place*
> *As droplets fell through the dark.*
> *Names printed on the ceiling of the night.*
> *Names slipping around a watery bend....*
> *Names written in the pale sky.*
> *Names rising in the updraft amid buildings.*
> *Names silent in stone or cried out behind a door.*
> *Names blown over the earth and out to sea....*
> *Names of citizens, workers, mothers and fathers,*
> *The bright-eyed daughter, the quick son.*
> *Alphabet of names in green rows in a field.*

---

46 Frank Rich, «We'll Win This War–On '24,'» *New York Times*, 9 Jan. 2005.
47 Coulter quoted in «Ms. Right,» *Time*, 25 April 2005.
48 Billy Collins, «The Names,» *New York Times*, 6 Sept. 2002.

Names in the small tracks of birds.
Names lifted from a hat
Or balanced on the tip of a tongue.
Names wheeled into the dim warehouse of memory.
So many names, there is barely room on the walls of the heart.

Thirty years earlier in the spring of 1971, as welders, plasterers, and electricians were completing work on the World Trade Center, Ali Ahmed Said, the informal poet laureate of the Arabs who is known throughout the Muslim world as Adonis, wrote «The Funeral of New York,» a very different kind of poem:[49]

Picture the earth as a pear
or breast.
Between such fruits and death
survives an engineering trick:
New York.
Call it a city on four legs
heading for murder
while the drowned already moan
in the distance.
New York is a woman
holding, according to history,
a rag called liberty with one hand
and strangling the earth with the other....
New York, you will find in my land
a bed and silence,
a chair, a head,
the sale of day and night,
the stone of Mecca
and the waters of the Tigris.
In spite of all this,
you pant in Palestine and Hanoi.
East and West you contend with people whose only history is fire....
Let statues of liberty crumble.
Out of corpses now sprout nails in the manner of flowers.
An eastern wind uproots tents and skyscrapers with its wings....

---

49 Adonis [Ali Ahmed Said], «The Funeral of New York,» in *The Pages of Day and Night*, trans. Samuel Hazo (Evanston, IL: Northwestern University Press, 1994), pp. 57–74. On Adonis' background, see Adam Shatz, «An Arab Poet Who Dares to Differ,» *New York Times*, 13 July 2002.

To cats and dogs the twenty-first century!
To people, extermination in this
the American century....
A clock announces time
while a letter comes from the east
written in a child's blood.
I scan it until the child's doll
becomes a cannon or a rifle.
Corpses in their streets make sisters
of Hanoi, Jerusalem, and Cairo....
Let our turn be now.
Let us be the executioners.
Let time keep floating on the sea of that equation:
New York plus New York equal a funeral.
New York minus New York equal the sun.

Adonis wrote his poem in Greenwich Village, less than two miles from Ground Zero. During his short stay in New York City, he made many American friends, but he was also outraged by American foreign policy. As Adonis saw it, Ho Chi Minh in Vietnam, Yasser Arafat in Palestine, and Gamal Abdel Nasser in Egypt were brothers in the struggle against American imperialism. Adonis had no time for the old American Century in 1971, nor has he any time for the Project for a New American Century today. This is something that the neo-conservatives in Washington need to ponder before they consider exporting regime change from Iraq to Syria or Iran in the months and years ahead. As one U.S. officer put it after the fall of Baghdad two years ago: «We're there. We're the dog that caught the car. Now what do we do with it?»[50] The Bush administration needs to answer this question pronto or we will almost certainly see more outbursts of anti-American terror in the Middle East and, perhaps, in the United States as well. Mark Twain understood the power of orientalism a hundred thirty-eight ago when the *S.S. Quaker City* arrived in the Eastern Mediterranean with a group of self-styled pilgrims on board. Americans have always wanted to remake the world in their own image, but they have always been profoundly ambivalent about the peoples to be remade. «The people stared at us every where, and we stared at them,» Twain concluded in *The Innocents Abroad*. «We generally made them feel rather small, too, before we got done with them, because we bore down on them with America's greatness until we crushed them.» This is the irony, and the tragedy, of American diplomacy in the Middle East.

---

50 Quoted in Todd S. Purdum, *A Time of Our Choosing: America's War with Iraq* (New York: Times Books, 2003), p. 6.

The United States and Israel: The Formative Years

Peter L. Hahn

This essay analyzes the origins and evolution of U.S.-Israeli relations in the 1940s and the 1950s. It shows that the questions pertaining to Israel generated enormous controversy within the United States. The controversy divided those officials who sympathized with the Zionist quest to establish and promote a Jewish state in Palestine from those who feared that such a development risked vital American interests in the Middle East. The essay will further show that such internal dynamics helped to shape an Israeli-U.S. relationship that was complicated and unstable. Despite a veneer of public friendship and a sense of democratic solidarity between the two states, American and Israeli officials quarreled frequently, and sometimes heatedly, on a variety of issues.

The Foundation of U.S.-Israeli Relations before 1948

The foundation of U.S.-Israeli relations was built by the Truman administration during the years preceding the Israeli declaration of statehood in 1948. During this period, the administration divided sharply on the issue of Jewish immigration to and statehood in Palestine. Officials in the State Department, the Pentagon, and the intelligence agencies opposed Zionism on security and diplomatic grounds. In light of the petroleum, military, transportation, and human resources of the Arab states, such officials deemed it essential to align the Arab states on the side of the West in the Cold War. American support of Zionism, they feared, would alienate the Arab states from the West and perhaps drive them into the arms of the Soviet Union.

Truman's personal advisers, by contrast, endorsed Zionism for political and humanitarian reasons. Public opinion among Christians and Jews widely supported the fulfillment of Zionist aspirations in Palestine, and Jewish Zionists comprised a powerful domestic political force. In addition, political liberals favored Jewish statehood as a means to serve the humanitarian interests of the post-Holocaust remnants of European Jewry. The conflicting advice that emanated from these two camps buffeted President Truman and directly shaped his inconsistent policy toward Zionism.

At three crucial junctures in 1945–1947, Truman ordered the implementation of pro-Zionist policy initiatives over the resistance of the security officials. In the first instance, the President endorsed the Zionist position on Jewish immigration to Palestine for humanitarian and domestic political reasons. He learned of the abysmal conditions in war refugee camps in Europe and the high costs of maintaining such facilities. Opinion polls showed that 78–80 percent of Americans who had followed the issue favored Jewish immigration to Palestine. In August 1945, Truman recommended to British Prime Minister Clement Attlee the admission of 100,000 Jewish refugees to Palestine in order to relieve suffering and ensure «future peace in Europe.» On September 29, a pending mayoral election in New York City, in which a Jewish Republican candidate vied for the traditionally Democratic Jewish vote, compelled Truman publicly to endorse the demand for 100,000 immigrants. On April 30, 1946, the President publicly supported a report by the Anglo-American Commission of Inquiry calling for admission of 100,000 Jewish immigrants to Palestine and he asked Britain to revoke the White Paper of 1939, a policy declaration in which Britain had pledged to restrict Jewish interests in Palestine and grant political independence to Arab Palestinians within ten years.[1]

Truman advanced Zionist aspirations a second time when he issued the so-called Yom Kippur statement on October 4, 1946. As the United Nations considered the partition of Palestine into a Jewish state and an Arab state, the President implicitly endorsed a Jewish state. Partition «would command the support of public opinion in the United States,» he declared. «… To such a solution our Government could give its support.» Truman's motives for issuing this statement have been widely debated. The President himself claimed purely humanitarian concerns. «I am not interested in the politics of the situation, or what effect it will have on votes in the United States,» he explained. «I am interested in relieving a half million people of the… distressful situation.» Most scholars, by contrast, agree with Kenneth Ray Bain's assessment that Truman's declaration was «a political statement designed for domestic consumption and promising little hope of winning immigration relief for the refugees.»[2]

Finally, Truman supported partition when the United Nations voted on the idea in November 1947. Consistent with their thinking since the early 1940s, policymakers in the State Department and Pentagon strongly opposed partition because they feared that it would eviscerate U.S. interests in the Arab world. But Truman, sympathetic to the survivors of Nazi

---

1 Truman to Attlee, 31 Aug. 1945: Harry S. Truman Papers, President's Secretary's File (PSF), Truman Library Subject File, boxes 184, 182. See also George H. Gallup, *Gallup Poll: Public Opinion 1935–1997*, (Wilmington, DE: Scholarly Resources, 2000), 554, 584; Henderson to Acheson, 4 Oct. 1945, General Records of the Department of State, National Archives (RG 59), Lot 54 D 403; Truman to Byrnes, 30 Apr. 1946, Harry S. Truman Papers White House Central File (WHFC-HST), Truman Library (Official), box 771.

2 Truman to Attlee with attachment, 3 Oct. 1946, *Foreign Relations of the United States: The Near East and Africa, 1946* (Washington: Government Printing Office, 1969) 8:701–703; Truman to George, 8 Oct. 1946, PSF, General File, box 138; Kenneth Bain, *March to Zion* (College Station: Texas A&M University, 1979) 136.

genocide and cognizant of the 2-to-1 support of partition in public opinion polls, fully supported partition on terms favorable to the prospective Jewish state. With U.S. backing, the General Assembly passed a partition resolution in November 1947.[3]

Although he took these three pro-Zionist steps, Truman refrained from unconditionally endorsing Zionism in 1945–1947. After calling for immigration of 100,000 Jews, for instance, the President refused Zionist entreaties to endorse a higher number. He declined to promote Zionist objectives during the mission of the United Nations Special Committee on Palestine (UNSCOP), and he criticized the reported, unofficial meddling by Zionists in the partition vote at the United Nations. The President privately articulated disquiet over the situation in Palestine and regret that domestic political pressures influenced foreign policy (even as he submitted to such factors). «We could have settled this Palestine thing if U.S. politics had been kept out of it,» he grumbled privately in May 1947. When a Chicago attorney warned that Truman's support for Palestinians would cost him the 1948 election, Truman privately complained that «it is drivels such as this that makes [sic] Anti-Semites.» The President also once remarked that he had received «35,000 pieces of mail and propaganda» from Zionists and that he «piled it up and put a match to it.»[4] Although his actions appeared pro-Zionist, Truman also harbored anti-Zionist impulses.

The Truman administration displayed a similar degree of ambivalence in its policy toward Israeli independence. In two crucial ways, the President lent vital assistance to the new State of Israel established on May 15, 1948. First, Truman formally recognized the Jewish state only minutes after its declaration of independence. He did so over the strong opposition of Secretary of State George C. Marshall, who suspected that Truman acted to advance domestic political interests but imperiled U.S. security objectives in the process.[5]

Second, Truman hampered a U.N. plan for ending the first Arab-Israeli war in 1948 on terms that Israel disapproved. Formulated by U.N. Mediator Count Folke Bernadotte, the plan proposed that the Arab states acquiesce in the existence of Israel, that Jordan annex the

---

3   State Department memorandum, 20 Sept. 1947, RG 59, Lot 54 D 403, box 9; CIG paper, 11 Sept. 1947, RG 59, 501.BB PALESTINE; JCS to Secretary of Defense, n.d. [c. 10 Oct. 1947], Record of the Joint Chiefs of Staff, National Archives (RG 218), CJCS Leahy, box 10, 056 Palestine; Statement by Marshall, *Foreign Relations of the United States, The Near East and Africa, 1947* (Government Printing Office, 1972) 5:1151; Gallup, *Gallup Poll*, 686–87; Eytan Gilboa, *American Public Opinion Toward Israel and the Arab-Israeli Conflict* (Lexington, Mass.: Lexington Books, 1987), 18–25.

4   Truman to Niles, 12 May 1947, Truman to Niles, 23 Aug. 1947, PSF, Subject File, box 184; Truman quoted in Edward Tivnan, *The Lobby: Jewish Political Power and American Foreign Policy* (New York: Simon and Schuster, 1987), 24. See also memorandum of conversation by Henderson, 19 June 1947, RG 59, Lot 53 D 444, box 11; Marshall to Truman, 10 July 1947, RG 59, Lot 54 D 403, box 9; Truman to Jacobson, 18 Oct. 1947, PSF, Subject File, box 184.

5   Epstein to Shertok, 14 May 1948, Israel State Archive, *Documents on the Foreign Policy of Israel* (DEP1), Jerusalem: Government Printer, 1981-97, 1:3–4; Epstein to Truman, 14 May 1948, Austin to Marshall, 19 May 1948, *Foreign Relations of the United States: The Near East, South Asia, and Africa, 1948*, (Washington: Government Printing Office, 1975), 5:989, 1013–15; Marshall to Epstein, 14 May 1948, RG 130.02, 2391/42.

portions of Palestine designated to Arab peoples, and that Israel repatriate Palestinian refugees. Although Israel and the Arab states indicated displeasure with the plan, the State Department endorsed and promoted it in September 1948 as a fair basis for settlement.[6]

In the heat of the 1948 election campaign, however, Truman scotched the Bernadotte plan under Israeli pressure. Israeli officials were alarmed that Democratic and Republican leaders suspended campaigning on foreign policy issues, because their silence enabled the State Department to promote Bernadotte's handiwork. Thus they encouraged the candidates of both parties to break their consensus and openly oppose the plan. Their efforts paid off in late October, when Republican nominee Thomas Dewey publicly censured it. Truman followed by pledging to reject key provisions of the plan, making it impossible for the State Department to sell it in the international realm.[7]

Despite Truman's recognition of Israel and scuttling of the Bernadotte plan, U.S. and Israeli leaders experienced hardship as they negotiated a major transition in their relationship. Accustomed to engaging in back channel diplomacy among pro-Zionists inside and outside the U.S. government, Israeli leaders found it difficult, after declaring statehood, to limit themselves to formal diplomatic channels. They faced an «influence dilemma,» an agonizing realization that their unofficial diplomacy – however successful it seemed at shaping U.S. policy – alienated top U.S. officials and thus weakened the formal U.S.-Israeli relationship.

For their part, U.S. officials haltingly came to grips with the new circumstance of Israeli sovereignty. Israel achieved statehood infused with nationalism, ready to pursue its national aims boldly, and reluctant to honor U.N. decrees or foreign directives. U.S. officials, by contrast, expected Israel to adhere to U.S. pressure and U.N. resolutions as if the new nation was still a mandate. They faced a «firmness dilemma,» thinking that firmness would compel Israel to submit to U.S. desires when in most cases it provoked Israeli defiance. That most State Department officials referred to Israeli territory as «Palestine» and to Israelis as «Jews» in late 1949 reveals willful or subconscious reluctance to accept the reality of Israel.

The influence and firmness dilemmas were aggravated by war-related issues that caused tensions between the United States and Israel. For example, Israeli officials insisted that they had a sovereign right to control immigration into their country. But the State Department affirmed Bernadotte's decision that immigration of men of military age violated the ceasefires, favored restrictions on Jewish immigration to Israel, and slowed the departure of Jewish men from Germany.[8]

---

6   Lovett to Truman, 18 Sept. 1948, Robert L. Dennison Papers, Truman Library, box 3. See also circular cable by Lovett, 19 Sept. 1948, RG 59, 501.BB PALESTINE.

7   Epstein to Shertok, 27 Sept. 1948, *DFPI*, 1:644–45; Weizmann to Jacobson, n.d. [Oct. 1948], Clifford Papers, box 13; Boyle to Connelly, 1 Oct. 1948, Barrows to Connelly, 1 Oct. 1948, Dennison Papers, box 3; Epstein to Silver, 14 Oct. 1948, Records of the Israeli Embassy in Washington, Israel State Archive, RG 93.08, 376/9; Clifford to Truman, 23 Oct. 1948, *FRUS, 1948*, 5:1509.

8   Marshall to Pinkerton, 26 May 1948, *FRUS, 1948*, 5:1057; Patterson to Marshall, 8, 13 July 1948, RG 59, 501.BB PALESTINE; Shertok to Weizmann, 20 July 1948, *DFPI*, 1:363–69.

Moreover, tensions developed between Israeli officials and U.S. military officers assigned as U.N. observers in Israel. An Army attaché reported that the observers were «unanimous in disgust at Jewish actions,» blamed the Israel Defense Forces (IDF) for ninety percent of truce violations, and considered Israeli officials «cocky, arrogant, wise guys, liars.» For their part, Israeli officials chafed at the very presence of U.N. officials in their country. «A large body of foreign people coming here to lay down the law on behalf of the U.N. went against the grain of the man in the street,» Foreign Minister Moshe Sharett told Bernadotte. «Why should Americans, Frenchmen, Belgians, and Swedes be coming here to boss us?... Why should we be treated as inferiors, when at long last we had achieved our independence?»[9]

Even President Truman limited his support of the new state in four important ways. First, he refused to provide weapons to the new state of Israel even though many observers predicted its doom. Backed by its domestic supporters, Israel pressed Truman for weapons during the first week of its independence, when Arab ground offensives and an Egyptian air raid on Tel Aviv made it anxious for warplanes and anti-aircraft guns. Obtaining arms was «a matter of life or death,» Sharett noted. There «were no words [to] express [the] desperate urgent need of planes.» Israel's envoy to the United Nations Abba Eban argued that the U.N. embargo, imposed in early 1948, had expired with the mandate and should not apply to sovereign Israel.[10]

State Department and Central Intelligence Agency (CIA) officers, however, convinced Truman that the embargo enhanced the prospect of a negotiated settlement by limiting the capacity of all powers to make war. If the United States armed Israel, the State Department cautioned, Arab states would sever relations with the West, curtail oil exports, and turn to Moscow for political assistance, and they might even use force to halt arms deliveries to Israel and thereby trigger U.S.-Arab war. With Truman's blessing, State Department officials enforced the embargo rigidly.[11]

Second, Truman allowed the State Department to dilute his recognition of the State of Israel. With Truman's approval, Assistant Secretary of State Robert Lovett clarified that the United States would withhold *de jure* recognition because Israel's borders were in flux and because communists might gain control of the government. The State Department also announced that envoy to Israel Charles F. Knox, Jr. would serve as special representative and not as minister or ambassador, and that it did not recognize the new government as the legal guardian of the Jews of Jerusalem. Truman approved these steps although some White House advisers cautioned that they would upset Israeli officials.[12]

---

9   Sanderson to Marshall, 27 Aug. 1948, RG 59, 501.BB PALESTINE; memorandum of conversation by Shertok, 10 Aug. 1948, Records of the Foreign Minister and Director-General of the Foreign Ministry, Israel State Archives, RG 130.02, 2443/2.
10 Shertok to Epstein, 22 May, 13 July 1948, *DFPI*, 1:59, 328.
11 NE paper, 27 May 1948, *FRUS, 1948*, 5:1060–61; paper by Merriam, 28 May 1948, RG 59, Lot 54 D 403, box 8.

Third, Truman occasionally expressed his disgust for the back channel lobbying conducted by Israeli officials. Israeli envoy Eliahu Epstein sensed that such efforts produced «undesirable complications» in his relations with the State Department. «Even loyal friends in Washington seem irritated, «Israeli Foreign Ministry officer Michael Comay added. Indeed, Marshall complained to Sharett on November 14 that Israel nurtured «both direct official contacts as between governments and indirect internal influence through American circles.» The United States would no longer tolerate back channel intrigues, he warned, but protest by recalling its envoy to Tel Aviv. Truman would not overrule Marshall on this point, a White House source told Epstein, because Lovett convinced him that national security was at stake.[13]

Once safely reelected in November, finally, Truman firmly discouraged Israeli military ventures against Egypt and Jordan. When Israel's incursion into Egypt briefly threatened to trigger an Anglo-Israeli war, the President quickly communicated to Israeli officials that they must withdraw their troops from the battlefield and rejected their pleas for support. «Public and official Washington opinion [is] dangerously tense, almost hostile» toward Israel, Epstein reported. Even Truman considered Israel a «troublemaker, endangering [the] peace by flouting [the] U.N.» In this context, Sharett assured the United States on January 1, 1949 that the IDF would retreat from Egypt, and the crisis abated.[14]

U.S.-Israeli relations, 1949–1953

In 1949–53, the United States and Israel developed a complex and ambiguous relationship. On the surface, the relationship appeared warm and friendly, as Israel garnered support and sympathy among key members of the Truman administration, members of Congress of both parties, and the U.S. public. At a deeper level, however, tension developed between the United States and Israel as the makers of foreign policy in both states clashed over several principles and issues. The clashes resulted from differences of policy on points of Arab-Israeli contention and on U.S.-Israeli bilateral issues.

Contemporary observers of the U.S.-Israeli relationship recorded evidence of warmth and friendliness. James G. McDonald, Truman's Special Representative (1948–49) and Ambassador (1949–51) to Israel, considered the Israeli people «markedly friendly,» while British Ambassador to Washington Oliver Franks reported that Israel «enjoys in the United States an unusual measure of Christian as well as Jewish goodwill.» On a visit to the United

---

12 Henderson to Lovett, 7 June 1948, RG 59, Lot 54 D 403, box 8; Marshall to Douglas, 3 July 1948, Marshall to Memminger, 10 July 1948, RG 59, 501.BB PALESTINE; Lovett to Forrestal, 8 July 1948, Records of the Office of the Secretary of Defense, National Archives, RG 330, CD 18–1–44.
13 Epstein to Eban, 5 Nov. 1948, note by Comay, 15 Nov. 1948, *DFPI*, 2:146–47, 181–83. See also Sharett to Elath, 19 Nov. 1948, Epstein to Sharett, 9 Dec. 1948, *DFPI*, 2:204–5, 281.
14 Epstein to Sharett, 6 Jan. 1949, *DFPI*, 2:347. See also Franks to Lovett, 29 Dec. 1948, RG 59, 767N.83; McDonald to Marshall, 5 Jan. 1949, RG 59, 501.BB PALESTINE.

States in 1951, Israeli Prime Minister David Ben-Gurion gained audiences with Truman, Acheson, Secretary of Defense George C. Marshall, and Truman's Special Assistant W. Averell Harriman and enjoyed enthusiastic receptions at numerous public appearances across the country. U.S. Jews and non-Jews, First Secretary of the Israeli embassy Esther Herlitz observed, «stand steadfastly at the right hand of Israel.»[15]

Israeli officials carefully cultivated U.S. goodwill. Cognizant of the importance of Truman's friendship, they encouraged him to assert his authority in U.S. policymaking. They appealed to his pride with such gestures as naming a recreation room at a disabled soldiers' hospital near Tel Aviv for his mother Martha Truman. «It seemed providential that Israel should have arisen» when Truman was President, Foreign Minister Moshe Sharett told him in person in July 1952. «We in Israel had felt all along that he was our true friend.»[16]

Israeli officials also nurtured ties with certain Presidential advisers whom they called their «friends in the White House.» David Niles, Truman's advisor on minority affairs, continued to brief Israeli envoys about policy developments within the White House and to lobby Truman on Israel's behalf. Ambassador McDonald divulged the internal dynamics of U.S. policy to Israeli officials and pressed Britain, France, Italy, and Greece to recognize Israel. «No better man could have been chosen by President Truman,» Ambassador Elath observed of McDonald. Harriman and Truman's friend Eddie Jacobson also advocated Israel's interests in the White House.[17]

Israeli officials also sought close relations with members of Congress. In February 1949, for instance, Israeli envoy Eliahu Elath hosted a dinner party for eight of the ten Jewish members of Congress, including such powerful representatives as House Judiciary Committee chair Emmanuel Cellar (D-New York), House Foreign Affairs Committee (HFAC) chair and 14-term representative Sol Bloom (D-New York), and HFAC members Jacob K. Javits (R-New York) and Abraham A. Ribicoff (D-Connecticut). Israeli envoys also secured the sup-

---

15 McDonald to Acheson, 5 Feb. 1949, RG 59, 711.67N; Franks to Bevin, 27 Apr. 1950, Political Correspondence of the Foreign Office, Public Record Office FO 371/82 523; report by Herlitz (Hebrew), 7 June 1951, RG 130.20, 2467/3. See also Eytan to Keren (Hebrew), 19 June 1950, Herlitz to Keren (Hebrew), 23 June 1950, Records of the U.S. Division, Foreign Ministry, Israel State Archive RG 130.20, 2479/8; Foreign Ministry paper (Hebrew), 3 June 1951, RG 130.20, 2479/9; Ben-Gurion to Truman, 31 May 1951, Truman to Ben-Gurion, 6 June 1951, RG 93.08, 337/1, 4; memorandum by Bendor (Hebrew), 19 July 1951, RG 130.20, 2467/4.

16 Minutes of meeting, 9 July 1951, *DFPI*, 6:450–52; memorandum of conversation by by Sharett, 1 July 1952, RG 130.20, 2474/27. See also memorandum by Bartley Crum, 2 Feb. 1950, PSF, Subject, box 181; note of an interview, [30 Aug. 1950], RG 130.20, 2464/8.

17 Elath to McDonald, 16 Mar. 1949, RG 93.08, 373/23. See also McDonald to Clifford, 16, 24 Aug. 1948, 11 June 1949, Clark M. Clifford Papers, Truman Library, box 13; Lourie to Eytan, 22 July 1949, Kollek to Keren (Hebrew), 30 June 1950, Keren to Kollek (Hebrew), 18 July 1950, Keren to USD (Hebrew), 23 May 1951, RG 130.20, 2479/8–9; Sharett to Niles, 18 Mar. 1951, RG 130.02, 2414/27; Kollek to Niles, 31 May 1951, Ben-Gurion to Harriman, 31 May 1951, David Ben-Gurion Papers, David Ben-Gurion Library, Correspondence File; Jacobson to Cohn, 1, 15 Apr. 1952, Chaim Weizmann Papers, Truman Library, box 1; Eban to Sharett (Hebrew), 21 Apr. 1952, RG 130.20, 2460/5.

port of non-Jewish members of Congress by encouraging their pro-Zionist constituents to express their opinions. When Senator Theodore F. Green (D-Rhode Island) criticized Israel in April 1952, Ambassador Abba Eban arranged a «flood of protests from Rhode Island» in response.[18]

Israeli officials also encouraged admiration of Israel in U.S. public opinion. The Foreign Ministry conceptualized a comprehensive information (*hasbara*) program in late 1949 to bolster Israel's image amidst criticisms of its policies on the refugees and Jerusalem issues. By 1950, Abraham Harman, the *hasbara* chief stationed in New York, organized visits of American notables to Israel, maintained close ties with U.S. labor leaders, and established posts in Israeli studies at U.S. universities. His staff claimed to influence editorials in U.S. newspapers, win the support of U.S. Christians, and shape film and television productions. Pro-Israel media pressure on the State Department during the Huleh controversy of 1951, Herlitz summarized, «shows you that it pays to have a press campaign.»[19]

While sympathy for Israel in the White House, Congress, and public opinion created a veneer of friendship toward Israel, a reservoir of resentment in the State and Defense Departments added a frosty edge to the relationship. The State Department remained alarmed that domestic pressure on Truman to support Israel threatened vital security interests in the Arab states. By June 1949, it monitored an «Israeli smear campaign» against department officials who resisted the pressure. In contrast to favorable public perceptions of Ben-Gurion, Navy Intelligence labeled him «a militant Zionist» who cavorted with Irgun and Stern Gang terrorists. U.S. military attaches in Tel Aviv reportedly mistrusted their Israeli contacts. Irritated by Israel's various conduits to the White House, officials in the Bureau of Near Eastern, South Asian, and African Affairs (NEA) provided Truman in June 1949 «a CIA report from Damascus relating to certain activities of Ambassador McDonald.» Within months, Truman authorized Acheson to recall McDonald.[20]

Acheson also resented the pro-Israel rhetoric of members of Truman's Cabinet. In a typical speech in 1950, for instance, Vice President Alben Barkley called Israel «an oasis of liberty in the desert of despotism.» Acheson's advisers concluded that such rhetoric stoked anger in the Arab states, manifest in bombings of U.S. legations in Beirut and Damascus, anti-U.S. statements by Arab leaders, and abstentions on U.N. resolutions regarding Korea. The secretary persuaded Truman to curtail his own pro-Israel rhetoric, but considered the speeches of Cabinet members a continuing problem.[21]

---

18 Eban to Sharett, 13 May 1952, RG 130.20, 2466/5. See also Epstein to Cellar, n.d. [Jan. 1949], RG 93.08, 366/26; Epstein to Shertok, 2 Feb. 1949, RG 130.20, 2479/10; Herlitz to Sharett (Hebrew), 8 Oct. 1950, RG 130.02, 2414/26; Keren to USD, 5 Jan. 1951, RG 130.20, 2479/8.
19 Herlitz to Levin, 8 June 1951, RG 130.20, 2479/9. See also Hahn, «The View From Jerusalem,» 525–27.
20 Humelsine to Acheson, 7 June 1949, RG 59, General Records of the Executive Secretariat, E394; memorandum by Sablalot, 15 May 1948, RG 330, CD 6–3–1; Humelsine to Acheson, 9 June 1949, RG 59, General Records of the Executive Secretariat, E394.

Israeli officials reciprocated the ill feelings in the State and Defense Departments but felt ensnared by the influence dilemma. Foreign Ministry Director-General Walter Eytan accused William J. Porter of the U.S. delegation at Lausanne of «abominable conduct» and Ben-Gurion found Acheson «rather stiff» at a May 1951 meeting. Worse, Truman became more deferential to the State Department after his reelection in 1948. «We cannot easily expect a repetition of events like the recognition of Israel by the fist of the President without his even consulting the Department of State,» embassy Counselor Moshe Keren observed in 1950. Although NEA posed a «bottleneck» to pro-Israel policy, Israeli officials realized, asking Truman to overrule it would inflame the situation.[22]

The tension between Israeli and U.S. diplomats stemmed not only from personal and political rivalry but also from a divergence in thinking about security issues. U.S. defense experts considered Israel an obstacle to regional stability upon which Western interests rested, and the National Security Council (NSC) grumbled about Israel's neutralism and «intensely nationalistic» character. For their part, the Israeli Foreign Ministry's United States Division (USD) resented «American interference and pressure in matters between us and our neighbors.» Because the United States aimed for «stability and peace» in the Middle East, they noted, «we are seen as a disruptive factor.... Israel is a 'bone in the throat'» of the United States.[23]

Indeed, U.S. and Israeli diplomats quarreled over several issues that lingered in the aftermath of the Arab-Israeli war. For instance, they squared off on territorial issues during the Lausanne peace conference of 1949. Israel indicated that it would retain Jaffa and western Galilee, territories that it had occupied beyond the partition borders. Truman, by contrast, declared that Israel must offer territorial compensation for all lands secured beyond the partition lines. At Lausanne, State Department envoys rejected an Israeli proposal to retain western Galilee and Jaffa without compensation. Mark Ethridge called Israel's refusal to heed U.S. policy «a slap in the face for the President» and «a declaration of intellectual warfare against the United States.» Angered by evidence that «certain agents of the Israeli Government» indirectly pressured Truman to relent, moreover, the State Department suggested «immediate adoption of a generally negative attitude toward Israel.»[24]

Soon, a battle for Truman's mind raged between the State Department and the Israeli government. Under-Secretary of State James E. Webb presented the President with a choice

---

21 Hare to Webb, 3 July 1950, *Foreign Relations of the United States: The Near East, South Asia, and Africa, 1950* (Washington: Government Printing Office, 1978), 5:947n.
22 Eytan to Sharett, 13 June 1949, minutes of meeting, 9 July 1951, Keren to USD, 24 Aug. 1950, *DFPI*, 4:121–28, 6:450–52, 5:493–97.
23 NSC 47/2, 17 Oct. 1949, *Foreign Relations of the United States: The Near East, South Asia, and Africa, 1949* (Washington: Government Printing Office, 1977) 6:1430–40; USD policy survey (Hebrew), n.d. [c. 1 Aug. 1950], RG 130.20, 2479/8.
24 Ethridge to Acheson, 10 June 1949, memorandum by Webb, 7 June 1949, State Department to Truman, 10 June 1949, *FRUS, 1949*, 6:1112–14, 1092, 1110.

between approving department policy on behalf of «our national interest» or overruling it in light of «strong opposition in American Jewish circles.» Afterward, Truman warned Ben-Gurion that his refusal to honor partition borders would force the United States to conclude «that a revision of its attitude toward Israel has become unavoidable.» When Webb reported Israeli efforts to pressure Truman through back channels, moreover, the President decided «to stand completely firm.» He told Jewish leaders who visited the White House on June 10 that «unless they were prepared to play the game fairly and conform to the rules they were probably going to lose one of their best friends.»[25]

Rather than buckle, Israeli leaders responded to Truman's message with firm diplomacy of their own. They argued that Arab aggression had invalidated the partition resolution and that Israeli security depended on occupation of territory beyond the partition lines. The Foreign Ministry also intensified its indirect pressure on Truman by «recruiting everybody we've got…, all the Baruchs, Crums, Frankfurters, Welles, young and old Roosevelts, etc., and making an all-out effort» to change Truman's mind. «No fair-minded man will deny us the right to retain that part of our ancient land,» Weizmann wrote to Truman, «which has become ours at a terrible cost of blood and treasure in the course of a war forced upon us by others.»[26]

Despite his initial firmness toward Israel, Truman soon caved in under the pressure from Israel and its domestic supporters. He backtracked from a State Department proposal that Israeli yield the southern Negev in exchange for its retention of Jaffa and Galilee. On August 19, Truman pledged to Eddie Jacobson, who visited the White House at Ambassador Eliahu Elath's behest, that «no single foot of land will be taken from Israel in [the] Negev.» Truman's change of heart forced Acheson to suspend pressure on Israel, wrecked the Lausanne conference, and further embittered the State Department against Israel.[27]

Second, U.S. and Israeli officials also sharply divided over the fate of the some 700,000 Palestinians who became refugees during the war. In spring 1949, Truman approved a State Department proposal that blended repatriation of some 250,000 refugees by Israel and resettlement of others by the Arab states. But the Israelis (as well as most Arab leaders) rejected the State Department's plan on security and political grounds. The refugees were «members of an aggressor group defeated in a war of its own making,» Ben-Gurion told Truman on 8 June. «Israel cannot in the name of humanitarianism be driven to commit suicide.» Israel also resisted the State Department plan by appealing to Truman through Truman's White House

---

25 Webb to Truman, 27 May 1949, PSF, Subject File, box 159, HSTL; Truman to Ben-Gurion, 28 May 1949, memorandum by Webb, 10 June 1949, *FRUS, 1949*, 6:1072–74, 1109.
26 Eytan to Sharett, 30 June 1949, Weizmann to Truman, 24 June 1949, *DFPI*, 4:186–89, 168–72.
27 Elath to Sharett, 19 Aug. 1949, *DFPI*, 4:375. See also Elath to Shiloah, 4 Aug. 1949, RG 93.08, 366/32; Ford to Acheson, 9 Aug. 1949, RG 59, 501.BB PALESTINE; Shiloah to Sharett (Hebrew), 9 Aug. 1949, Elath to Clifford, 15 Aug. 1949, *DFPI*, 4:303, 352–57; circular cable by Acheson, 16 Aug. 1949, *FRUS, 1949*, 6:1316–18.

aides; U.S. Jewish journalists, lobbyists and fund-raisers; and Ambassador to Tel Aviv James B. McDonald.[28]

Again, the State Department and the State of Israel battled for Truman's mind. Bothered by evidence of Israel's indirect pressure on him, Truman told Webb «that he has no doubt as to the wisdom of the course being followed» by the State Department. The United States «is seriously disturbed by the attitude of Israel,» Truman told Ben-Gurion. If Israel remained inflexible, the administration «will regretfully be forced to the conclusion that a revision of its attitude toward Israel has become unavoidable.» Truman authorized an aide-memoire to Israel on 24 June that called the refugee problem «a common responsibility of Israel and the Arab States, which neither side should be permitted to shirk.»[29]

Israel's resistance to the American pressure to absorb 250,000 refugees triggered a diplomatic brouhaha that snowballed into a U.S.-Israeli crisis. Sharett arranged for one of Truman's aides, General John Hilldring, to discern if the President would approve a deal in which Israel absorbed 100,000 refugees. Truman told Hilldring that he probably would approve such a deal, but he also admonished Hilldring not to notify the Israelis. But Hilldring relayed the news to Sharett, who floated the 100,000 idea to the State Department with the claim that Truman had approved it. The State Department rejected the offer, warned Israeli officials not to tamper with the U.S. policymaking process, and alerted Truman that the aide had betrayed his trust.[30]

Truman reacted angrily to the Israeli ploy. He promptly suspended the $49 million balance of Israel's $100 million Export-Impost Bank loan and approved other such measures against Israel. «I would be less than frank,» he wrote to Weizmann, «if I did not tell you that I was disappointed.» Israeli officials complained that the aid suspension «cut across the type of relationship... which should exist between Israel and the United States.»[31]

Third, a major debate on the status of Jerusalem generated tension between the United States and Israel. Jordan and Israel, which had occupied the city during the war, insisted on de facto division of it between them. U.S. officials, by contrast, favored some type of international control under U.N. auspices. Israeli officials followed their usual course of appealing to Truman to overturn the State Department's policy. Having anticipated such a move,

---

28 Israeli aide-memoire, 8 June 1949, *FRUS, 1949*, 6:1102–6. See also circular cable by Acheson, 29 Apr. 1949, *FRUS, 1949*, 6:959–60; Elath to Sharett, 27 May 1949, Eban to Sharett, 1 June 1949, Kollek to Sharett, 10 June 1949, *DFPI*, 4:71–72, 88, 115–17; Kollek to Eban, 6 June 1949, RG 130.02, 2443/3.

29 Memorandum of conversation by Webb, 31 May 1949, RG 59, General Records of the Executive Secretariat, E394; Webb to McDonald, 28 May 1949, *FRUS, 1949*, 6:1072–74; U.S. aide-memoire, n.d. [24 June 1949], PSF, Subject File, box 184.

30 Eban to Eytan, 24 June 1949, Heyd to Herlitz, 1 July 1949, *DFPI*, 4:165–67, 194–96; Lourie to Eytan, 22 July 1949, RG 130.20, 2479/8; Acheson to McDonald, 16 Aug. 1949, *FRUS, 1949*, 6:1321; Porter to Acheson, 3 August 1949, Clifford Papers, box 14, Truman Library.

31 Truman to Weizmann, 13 Aug. 1949, *FRUS, 1949*, 6:1305–8; Elath to Sharett, 2 Sept. 1949, *DFPI*, 4:424.

Acheson preemptively secured the President's explicit approval of international control. Unfortunately for Acheson, the United Nations approved an extreme plan for internationalization that even he considered impractical.[32]

U.S. and Israeli officials also quarreled about the transfer of Israeli Government Offices to Jerusalem. In reaction to the United Nations action, Ben-Gurion moved the Office of Prime Minister to Jerusalem in December 1949 as a means of asserting Israeli sovereignty there. State Department officials criticized the move «as open opposition by Israel to the United Nations» and indicated that they would not move the U.S. Embassy to Jerusalem or conduct any official business there. Yet U.S. officials also found it impossible to reverse Ben-Gurion's move.[33]

In addition to this divergence of thinking on points of Arab-Israeli contention, U.S.-Israeli relations also experienced strain over differences on various bilateral issues. In late 1948, for example, Israel sought U.S. *de jure* recognition, and Special Counsel Clark Clifford, McDonald, and various members of Congress endorsed the request. After Marshall emphasized that the U.S. *de facto* recognition of May 1948 had alienated the Arab states, however, Truman hesitated. He recognized Israel only after a permanent government was elected in January 1949 and, to Israel's displeasure, he simultaneously recognized Jordan.[34]

U.S. and Israeli officials also sparred briefly on the question of Israeli membership in the United Nations. Truman accepted Clifford's reasoning that Israel deserved a U.N. seat like several Arab states had, and he directed Acheson to support its request for membership. With U.S. support, the Security Council approved a resolution affirming Israeli membership in March 1949. But then Acheson, angry at Israel's «liberal use of big stick in armistice talks,» sought to delay its U.N. admission to demonstrate that it «cannot continue to ignore with impunity [the] opinion [of the] world community.» Truman agreed and authorized Acheson to bury the Israeli petition in a General Assembly committee.[35]

Israel, however, again waged a triumphant battle for Truman's mind. Elath mobilized certain «White House friends» to argue to the President that Israel was more likely to cooperate with U.N. peacemaking initiatives as a member. Truman also reasoned, Acheson noted, that a reversal of the U.S. endorsement of December 1948 would cause «confusion and irri-

---

32 McDonald to Clifford, 30 Nov. 1949, Clifford Papers, box 13; Elath to Eytan, 24 Nov., 2 Dec. 1949, *DFPI*, 4:646, 674; Acheson to Truman, 21 Nov. 1949, *FRUS, 1949*, 6:1498–99; memorandum of conversation by Acheson, 21 Nov. 1949, RG 59, General Records of the Executive Secretariat, E394.
33 Hare to Acheson, 17 Dec. 1949, *FRUS, 1949*, 6:1547–48; State Department policy paper, «Israel,» 6 Feb. 1951, memorandum of conversation by McGhee, 11 Jan. 1950, *Foreign Relations of the United States: The Near East and Africa, 1951* (Washington: Government Printing Office, 1982), 5: 570–77, 682–84.
34 Bloom to Truman, 3 Aug. 1948, Cellar to Truman, 4 Aug. 1948, PSF, Subject File, box 184; Marshall to Truman, 23 Aug. 1948, RG 59, Lot 54 D 403, box 8; McDonald to Truman, 18 Jan. 1949, Clifford Papers, box 14; Elath to Sharett, 24 Jan. 1949, *DFPI*, 2:395; Acheson to Truman, 27 Jan. 1949, WHCF-HST (Official), box 775.
35 Burdett to Acheson, 20 Apr. 1949, *FRUS, 1949*, 6:923n, 927–30.

tation» against the administration and that supporting Israel's admission might gain leverage over the country. On 11 May, the General Assembly passed a U.S.-cosponsored resolution to admit Israel.[36]

U.S. and Israeli officials also squabbled over a loan from the Export-Import Bank to Israel. Once Israel held elections and signed the armistice agreements in early 1949, the State Department approved a $100 million loan bank loan to Israel. With Truman's approval, however, Acheson ordered bank officials to sequester the loan's $49 million balance in August 1949 because of Israel's policy toward Palestinian refugees. Israel complained to Truman, via Niles, of the State Department's «coercion and blackmail,» and Acheson, feeling pressured by the White House, capitulated. He approved allocations of $2.4 million in late August and $20 million in October even though Israel remained unyielding on the refugees issue.[37]

The U.S. relationship with Israel displayed both accord and discord in 1949–1953. Israel enjoyed the friendly support of President Truman, the White House staff, Congress, and influential private citizens in the United States. Much of this support derived from the traditional pro-Zionism of the White House and public opinion, while some of it resulted from the conscious efforts by Israeli officials to mobilize its so-called «friends» in the United States. By contrast, professionals in the State and Defense Departments remained suspicious of Israel, which they viewed as an impediment to their goal of a stable and pro-Western Arab world.

Such tensions within the administration shaped the resolution of such diplomatic issues as Arab-Israeli disputes and U.S.-Israeli bilateral issues. In each case, State Department professionals preferred to extract certain concessions as the price of favorable U.S. policy. But Truman, sensitive to domestic pressures, ultimately ordered enactment of policies that provided Israel what it wanted. As in the disputes over borders, refugees, and Jerusalem, Israel's lobbying of Truman stoked anger among State Department officials, revealing the risks to Israel inherent in the influence dilemma.

U.S.-Israeli relations, 1953–1961

U.S. relations with Israel continued to experience instability during the presidency of Dwight D. Eisenhower. To correct a perceived pro-Israel disposition of the Truman government, the Eisenhower administration sought to practice impartiality on all Arab-Israeli questions. Israeli officials naturally resisted this shift, and discord resulted from U.S. policy on specific Arab-Israeli conflicts, initiatives to promote Arab-Israeli peace, and other issues.

---

36 Elath to Sharett, 10 May 1949, *DFPI*, 4:38–39; Acheson to Ethridge, 12 May 1949, *FRUS, 1949*, 6:1004–5.
37 Elath to Sharett, 25 Aug. 1949, *DFPI*, 4:396–97. See also Rockwell to Acheson, 10 Sept. 1949, *FRUS, 1949*, 6:1375; Elath to Sharett, 26 Aug. 1949, *DFPI*, 4:400.

Official relations declined dramatically during the Suez-Sinai War of 1956–57 and the Lebanon-Jordan crisis of 1958. Although Israel maintained deep reservoirs of sympathy in U.S. public opinion, fissures opened in U.S.-Israeli official relations.

U.S.-Israeli relations were shaken in 1953 by Eisenhower's impartiality policy. Cognizant that their political fortunes were relatively immune from the pro-Israeli lobby, Eisenhower and Dulles agreed to practice «a policy of *true* impartiality» between Israel and Arab states. To Israeli diplomats, this shift in U.S. policy caused «great confusion…, nervousness and agitation…. The Administration is not particularly responsive to Israel's position and there is no longer a Mr. Truman to pick up the telephone and order something done regardless of the consequences.»[38]

Israel softened the impartiality policy by recruiting U.S. politicians to challenge it, but the tension remained. In 1953, Israeli envoys mobilized U.S. Jews to lobby members of Congress to pressure Eisenhower, and Ambassador to Washington Abba Eban persuaded prominent Democrat Adlai Stevenson to reject the President's request to affirm impartiality in the spirit of bipartisanship. Bowing to such political pressures, Dulles assured Eban on 8 October 1953 that the U.S. government and people «ascribed to their friendship with Israel a special importance.» But Ben-Gurion suspected that «America wants in fact a mandate on Israel» and resolved that «we must keep our sovereignty which is a condition of our existence.»[39]

A relative decline in the influence of the Israel lobby added to Israel's frustration. State Department officials questioned the American Zionist Committee's tax-exempt status because of the political lobbying it conducted. In 1954, its chief I.L. Kenen created the American Zionist Committee for Public Affairs (renamed the American Israel Public Affairs Committee in 1959), which, lacking tax-exempt status, remained under-funded for years. Because U.S. officials complained that meeting individual Jewish leaders demanded too much time, moreover, various Jewish groups formed the Conference of Presidents of Major American Jewish Organizations in 1954. Conference members collectively met Eisenhower on occasion but found their effectiveness limited by the need to arrive at a consensus before each visit. Ambivalence among members of the group about certain of Israel's policies–such as its raids at Qibya and Gaza and its invasion of Egypt – also limited its effectiveness as a pro-Israel lobby.[40]

Israeli leaders also regretted a slight decline in support for Israel among the U.S. people. In early 1957, the Gallup poll found that 33 percent of Americans held a favorable view of Israel, 53 percent were neutral, and 14 percent held unfavorable views. While popular atti-

---

38 Memorandum by Dulles, 1 June 1953, RG 59, Lot 64 D 563, box 30; memorandum of conversation by Goitein, 6 Mar. 1953, RG 130.20, 2460/6; Avner to Bender, 9 Sept. 1953, 130.20, 2475/2.
39 Eban memorandum, 8 Oct. 1953, ISA, RG 130.20, 2460/6; Ben-Gurion Diary (Hebrew), 2, 11 July 1954.
40 Tivnan, *The Lobby*, 37–50; David Goldberg, *Foreign Policy and Ethnic Interest Groups: American and Canadian Jews Lobby for Israel* (New York: Greenwood Press, 1990), 15–17.

tudes toward Arab states were much less friendly, only 10 percent of Americans approved Israel's attack on Egypt in October 1956 and 47 percent disapproved. Fifty percent expressed satisfaction with Eisenhower's handling of the Israeli-Egyptian clash – which included pressure on Israel to withdraw from the Sinai and Gaza – and only 23 percent voiced dissatisfaction.[41]

At a fundamental level, relations between the United States and Israel were strained by their conflicting views of the Arab states. In the interest of anti-Soviet containment, U.S. officials sought to maintain influence among Arab powers, downplayed the seriousness of Arab threats to eliminate Israel, and called upon Israel to achieve peace by making certain concessions. Israel, by contrast, interpreted Arab propaganda and arms acquisitions as serious threats to its security, used force to secure its borders, and demanded U.S. political support and arms supply. As a measure of the gulf between the two powers, Prime Minister Moshe Sharett justified Israel's raid in Gaza in February 1955 as «an act of self-defense of a beleaguered nation surrounded by enemies,» while NEA argued that «such raids make the whole border situation worse and not better.» When the State Department pressed Ben-Gurion to make peace by conceding territory to Arab states, he replied that «as long as we live we will not permit anyone to rob us of a single inch of our land.»[42]

Disagreement over a prospective U.S. guarantee of Israeli security further strained U.S.-Israeli relations. Disturbed that U.S. security schemes such as the Middle East Defense Organization, the Baghdad Pact, and the Eisenhower Doctrine enhanced the military capabilities of their Arab adversaries, Israeli leaders sought an explicit U.S. security guarantee. But Eisenhower refused their requests on the grounds that such a provision would anger Arab leaders, distract them from the Soviet menace, and thereby undermine vital Western interests.[43]

Eisenhower's initiative in the late 1950s to mend his relationship with Nasser also strained his relationship with Israel. Israeli officials relentlessly pressed the State Department to abandon the U.S. rapprochement with the United Arab Republic (UAR) on the grounds that Nasser's political adventurism in neighboring states destabilized the region. Minister to Washington Yaacov Herzog expressed concern «lest improved U.S.-U.A.R. relations should be at the expense of Israel,» and *hasbara* officials made plans to «raise hell» in U.S. public opinion on the issue. But State Department officials rejected the argument that improvement in U.S.-UAR relations would hurt Israel.[44]

---

41 Gallup, *Gallup Poll*, 1454–57, 1464, 1484–85; Gilboa, *American Public Opinion*, 32–33.
42 Sharett to Dulles, 12 April 1955, RG 59, 601A.86; Jernegan to Dulles, 13 April 1955, RG 59, 601.84A11; Lawson to Dulles, 17 Nov. 1955, RG 59, 684A.86.
43 Circular telegram by Dulles, 24 Aug. 1955, RG 59, 684A.86; Shiloah to Eban (Hebrew), 10 Feb. 1958, Records of the Foreign Ministry, Central Registry, Political Files, Israel State Archive, RG 130.23, 3088/6; Dulles to Eisenhower, 5 Mar. 1958, Dwight D. Eisenhower Papers (Ann Whitman File), Eisenhower Library (DDE), box 7; Eban to Meir (Hebrew), 11 Oct. 1958, summary of discussion (Hebrew), 1 Dec. 1958, Eliav to Eban (Hebrew), 6 April 1959, Eban to Eliav (Hebrew), 28 April 1959, RG 130,23, 3088/6–7.

The Arab factor also caused U.S.-Israeli discord on arms supply. Israel repeatedly requested U.S. weapons supply in 1953–56, especially during what Eban called the «solemn hour of national emergency» following the Soviet-Egyptian arms deal of 1955. Convinced that Israel had the capability to defeat its adversaries, however, the State Department calculated that arming Israel would alienate Arab states and ruin prospects for a permanent peace settlement. Arming Israel «would be fatal to our position in the Middle East,» William M. Rountree of NEA observed, because «the result would be a tiny Israel armed by the U.S. opposed to the Arab world supported by the Soviet bloc.»[45]

U.S. arms supply policy continued to generate discord as the Soviets supplied weapons to Arab powers in the late 1950s. Citing their need to deter or thwart Arab attack, Israeli officials demanded substantial quantities of U.S. weapons, including tanks, aircraft, and anti-aircraft missiles. The U.S. reply, Ben-Gurion told Eisenhower, would determine whether the Israelis «were to remain a free, independent nation or whether they were going to be exterminated.» Except for token arms sales in 1958 and 1960, however, Eisenhower refused Israeli requests on the grounds that he would trigger a Middle East arms race and encourage deeper Soviet-Arab ties.[46]

In the twilight of Eisenhower's presidency, U.S.-Israeli relations were further strained by Israel's nuclear program. U.S. intelligence confirmed in September 1960 that Israel had secretly constructed at Dimona a nuclear reactor capable of producing weapons-grade plutonium. Eisenhower's fears of a nuclear arms race in the Middle East were confirmed when Nasser declared in December that if Israel built an atomic bomb then the «UAR would get one, too, at any price.» U.S. officials expressed to Israel that they «unequivocally opposed» nuclear proliferation in the Middle East and that Israel should allow international inspections to confirm Israel's claim that the Dimona reactor was devoted to peaceful purposes. Eisenhower remained troubled by Ben-Gurion's equivocal answer.[47]

While such security issues generated a climate of tension, U.S.-Israeli relations hit bottom twice during the Eisenhower years. During the Suez-Sinai War, Eisenhower called Israel «an aggressor,» endorsed U.N. resolutions censuring Israel, and threatened to impose sanctions. The United States had «no moral reason to condemn our action... of self-defence,» Ben-Gurion retorted, since it «has not experienced the nightmare of continuous aggression

---

44   Memorandum of conversation by Jones, 16 Dec. 1959, RG 59, 684A.86B; Avnon to Herzog (Hebrew), 27 July 1959, RG 130.23, 3089/10; State Department position paper, 5 March 1960, Dwight D. Eisenhower Papers (White House Central File), Eisenhower Library (Confidential), box 79.
45   Eban to Dulles, 31 Jan. 1956, RG 130.20, 2480/9; Makins to Foreign Office, 10 Sept. 1953, FO 371/104 240; Rountree to Dulles, 8 June 1956, RG 59, 611.84A.
46   Memorandum of conversation, 10 Mar. 1960, White House Office Files, Eisenhower Library, Office of Staff Secretary, International Seires, box 8.
47   Reinhardt to Herter, 24 Dec. 1960, Merchant to Reid, 31 Dec. 1960, *Foreign Relations of the United States: Arab-Israeli Dispute; United Arab Republic; North Africa, 1958–1960* (Washington: Government Printing Office, 1992), 13: 609–11, 399–400.

and the threat of extinction as we have.» Eisenhower delayed sanctions because congressional and public opinion supported Israel, but only Ben-Gurion's decision to withdraw his forces from Gaza and Sinai enabled U.S.-Israeli relations to avoid further decline.[48]

During the crises in Lebanon and Jordan in 1958, even deeper disharmony gripped U.S.-Israeli relations as officials in Washington sensed that Israel had become a liability to their anti-Soviet containment policy. As Marines occupied Beirut, Dulles lamented that «Israel is a hostage held against us» by Soviet-supported Arab nationalists. He and Eisenhower justified intervention in Lebanon and Jordan as applications of dual containment, to deny the countries to Nasserite radicals and to Israel. Eisenhower agreed that «except for Israel we could form a viable policy in the area,» although he wondered «how to take a sympathetic position regarding the Arabs without agreeing to the destruction of Israel.» In August, by contrast, when the NSC identified U.S. «bedrock objectives» in the Middle East, meaning interests worth fighting to protect, Eisenhower clarified that «preserving the independence of Israel should not be added to our bedrock objectives at this time.»[49]

The NSC seriously reconsidered relations with Israel in November 1958. It identified Soviet expansionism «using Arab nationalism as its instrument» as the chief danger in the Middle East. To counteract it, the United States must build bridges to estranged Arab states, seek an Arab-Israeli compromise peace settlement, and discourage extra-regional arms supply. To deter Israel from upsetting their plans, U.S. officials should «make clear as appropriate that, while U.S. policy embraces the preservation of the State of Israel in its essentials, we believe that Israel's continued existence as a sovereign state depends on its willingness to become a finite and accepted part of the Near East nation-state system.»[50]

Israeli officials sensed this shift in U.S. thinking. The Foreign Ministry extensively discussed what it called the «crisis with the U.S.,» which, overlooking the deeper U.S. uncertainties about the value of Israel, it attributed to U.S. anger at Israel for suspending the overflights to Jordan. Some Israeli officials believed that «the anger was worthwhile;... it shook up the Americans a little bit and reminded them that it is not so simple to deal with us.» But most of them worried that U.S. irritation would persist indefinitely and permeate even Congress and the public. «We gained nothing from the crisis,» Herzog noted, «and it would be better if it had not happened at all.»[51]

---

48 Minutes of NSC meeting, 1 Nov. 1956, *Foreign Relations of the United States: Suez Canal Crisis, 1955–1957* (Washington: Government Printing Office, 1990), 16:907; Ben-Gurion to Smith, 2 Jan. 1957, Ben-Gurion Papers, Correspondence File.

49 Memorandum of conversation by Goodpaster, 24 July 1958, Whitman File: Diary Series, box 35; minutes of NSC meeting, 21 Aug. 1958, *Foreign Relations of the United States: The Near East Region; Iraq; Iran; Arabian Peninsula, 1958–1960* (Washington: Government Printing Office, 1993), 12: 154–56.

50 NSC 5820/1, 4 Nov. 1958, Records of the National Security Council, National Archives, RG 273. See also minutes of NSC meeting, 16 Oct. 1958, Whitman File: NSC Series, box 10.

51 Avner to Hertzog (Hebrew), 12 Aug. 1958, and Hertzog to Avner (Hebrew), 21 Aug. 1958, RG 130.23, 3088/6.

In the aftermath of the 1958 crises, U.S.-Israeli relations stabilized as U.S. officials reaffirmed the impartiality policy. «We seek to treat Israel like any other friendly state,» NEA officials resolved. «The interests of special groups in this country in Israel must be taken into account, but our policy must be based primarily on our national interests in the area, where there are other states with which we desire firm and friendly relations.» Israel «occupies a very special place in U.S. international relations,» Rountree instructed Ambassador-designate to Tel Aviv Ogden Reid in June 1959, but the «very close relationship with Israel has to be carefully balanced by our attention to the Arab states.»[52]

The tension in official U.S. policy toward Israel was reflected in private expressions by U.S. officials about Israeli leaders. Michelle Mart has suggested that the United States revealed a preference for Israel by casting its people in favorable, masculine terms and the Arab people in unfavorable, feminine terms. U.S. officials, however, routinely feminized Israeli leaders. Ambassador to Tel Aviv Edward B. Lawson reported, for example, that Ben-Gurion was «emotionally upset and... near to tears» on a certain issue and in general «subject more to emotional than intellectual influences.» For the same derisive effect, U.S. officials described Foreign Minister Golda Meir in masculine terminology. «She can out-Arab the Arabs,» Donald C. Bergus of NEA once noted, «when it comes to the almost irresponsible use of strong language.»[53] Clearly, U.S.-Israeli official relations remained less than special through the 1950s.

U.S.-Israeli relations remained strained through the 1950s by differences over Arab-related issues. Israeli leaders disliked the Eisenhower administration's impartiality, its mediation of Arab-Israeli disputes, and its deliberate efforts to mollify Nasser and King Saud. They calculated that they should pursue arms supply, security assurances, and other strategic concessions from the United States in order to neutralize the mortal danger posed by the Arab states. By contrast, U.S. officials found Israel's security demands incompatible with their own Cold War interests in the Arab world. They disputed Israel's views on arms supply, security commitments, and Arab-Israeli conflicts.

Israeli officials perceived this dichotomy in the relationship. At the bilateral level, Eliav observed in September 1959, «everything is usually all right because there are many factors, spiritual, public, and even political that work for this friendship.» At the multilateral level, however, U.S.-Arab and Israeli-Arab dynamics strained U.S.-Israeli relations because the United States took a position of «neutrality» toward Israel. «It is clear that there is a gap between these two levels and the American attempts to bridge them are impossible.» Although U.S.-Israeli bilateral relations were sound and the U.S. public liked Israel, Ben-

---

52 Rockwell to Rountree, 9 June 1959, RG 59, Lot 61 D 43, box 2; memorandum of conversation by Hamilton, 11 June 1959, RG 59, 611.84A.
53 Lawson to Dulles, 29 Feb. 1956, RG 59, 684A.86; Lawson to Dulles, 20 Apr. 1956, RG 59, 674.84A; Bergus to Lawson, 16 Mar. 1957, RG 59, Lot 59 D 582, box 4. See also Mart, «Tough Guys and American Cold War Policy.»

Gurion noted in 1960, trouble occurred whenever the United States thought of Israel in its Middle East context, because Arab interests weighed in.[54]

Conclusion

This essay argues that the U.S.-Israeli relationship in the 1940s and 1950s was controversial and complicated. The evidence presented in this paper suggests, indeed, that Israel generated major differences of opinion among U.S. officials and between the executive and legislative branches of the U.S. government. Some American officials emphasized the strategic costs of backing Israel while others stressed the domestic political, ideological, and humanitarian costs of not supporting the Jewish state. Such different perspectives and priorities led to constant disagreement about the proper American disposition toward Israel.

As a result, a complex U.S.-Israeli relationship developed through the 1950s. On the one hand, Israel enjoyed widespread support among the American people, in Congress, and in certain parts of the executive branch, such as the White House staff and occasionally the Oval Office itself. Israeli officials made special effort to nurture and encourage such support, sensing that their very national survival depended on it. This pro-Zionist, pro-Israeli disposition ensured that the United States would offer Israel vital support at decisive moments and that the United States would not pull the plug on the Israeli experiment in statehood.

On the other hand, there persisted in the U.S. foreign policy bureaucracy a countervailing impulse to limit support of Israel on behalf of American security interests in the Middle East. Thus U.S. officials continuously pressed Israel to make peace with its Arab neighbors by making concessions to them, and they eschewed arms deals, security commitments, and other political connections that would earn Arab reproach of the United States. The Israeli influence dilemma and the U.S. firmness dilemma only added to the tension that resulted from policy differences. Through the 1950s, the U.S.-Israeli relationship experienced a mixture of friendliness and tension, amity and discord.

Some scholars have characterized the American-Israeli relationship as a «special relationship» since its birth. These scholars, including some who applaud the close relationship and others who censure it, accentuate evidence of close American support for Israel and deep sympathy for Israel in U.S. public opinion.[55] Some even suggest that the relationship was mystical. While the nature of that relationship in later decades is a topic for another essay, the U.S.-Israeli relationship displayed too much tension through the 1950s to qualify as a «special relationship.»

---

54 Eliav to Eban (Hebrew), 21 Sept. 1959, RG 130.23, 3088/7. See also Ben-Gurion Diary (Hebrew), 2 Jan. 1960.
55 Bernard Reich, *Quest for Peace: United States-Israel Relations and the Arab-Israel Conflict* (New Brunswick: Transaction Books, 1977); Dan Raviv and Yossi Melman, *Friends in Deed: Inside the U.S.-Israel Alliance* (New York: Hyperion, 1994); Alexandre Safran, *Israel in Time and Space* (New York: Feldheim, 1987); George W. Ball Douglas B., *The Passionate Attachment: America's Involvement with Israel, 1947 to the Present* (New York: Norton, 1992); Cheryl Rubenberg, *Israel and the American National Interest* (Urbana: University of Illinois Press, 1986).

Oil, Allies, Anti-communism, and Nationalism:
U.S. Interests in the Middle East since 1945

Mary Ann Heiss

Strategically located at the juncture of Asia, Africa, and Europe, the Middle East became increasingly important in U.S. diplomatic calculations after the Second World War. Largely content before the war to play a supporting role in regional affairs, after 1945 U.S. officials repeatedly pushed their way into the Middle East and came to exert ever more influence on developments there. Beyond its crucial strategic position, though, the region also attracted U.S. attention because of its rich – in fact, unparalleled – petroleum supplies. U.S. policymakers derived from World War II a renewed appreciation of their country's dependence on foreign petroleum resources and a heightened awareness of petroleum's importance to the security of the United States and its Western allies. The region therefore had to be protected from Soviet encroachment – and later, indigenous nationalism – at virtually all costs. As events ultimately played out, however, at times the cost of protecting the region included sacrificing U.S. relations with the very nations that joined the United States in the Western alliance. This essay is designed to illustrate, through reference to selected instances of U.S. intervention in the Middle East since 1945, how oil, allies, and opposition to communism and/or nationalism intersected in U.S. regional policy. In the process, I hope to illuminate Washington's shifting priorities during the Cold War and after, as well as the multiplicity of considerations that often came together to shape U.S. policy and the way that U.S. decisions regarding the Middle East affected relations with other nations outside the region.

The Anglo-Iranian oil dispute of the early 1950s was one of the first post-World War II problems to confront U.S. policymakers in the Middle East. Although not a direct participant in the dispute, Washington ultimately stepped in to facilitate a resolution and therefore played an important role in the nationalization crisis almost from the start. For the British, the nationalization crisis threatened their traditional control over Iranian oil and imperiled their other international investments as well. (During World War I, the British government had purchased a large amount of stock in the Anglo-Persian Oil Company; by 1950 it held slightly more than half – or a controlling interest – in its successor, the Anglo-Iranian Oil Company [AIOC].) To counteract the dangers inherent in Iran's nationalization, British officials pursued a hard-line policy that would limit Iranian gains and ensure continued British control of Iranian oil. For the Americans, the main danger in Iran was the possibility that the oil dispute would destabilize the Iranian economy and lead to Soviet advances throughout the Middle East. To prevent such an eventuality, the Americans initially advocated a moderate course that would assuage Iranian nationalism without surrendering that country – and its oil – to Communist control. Over time, though, they abandoned that strategy in favor of a joint Anglo-American front that quashed Iranian nationalism, ensured continued Western control of Iranian oil, including a new stake for U.S. companies, and protected important Western interests. Although the British and the Americans ultimately joined forces, the Iranian nationalization crisis revealed the different priorities that motivated policymakers in London and Washington. It also presaged the serious disagreements that would divide the Atlantic allies during the 1956 Suez debacle.

Iran's nationalization of the AIOC stemmed from fifty years of dissatisfaction with the company's near domination of Iran's economy and society. In 1949, the Iranians had tried to better their financial return from the AIOC by negotiating a new concession agreement. Although the resulting Supplemental Oil Agreement would dramatically increase Iran's oil receipts, it did not go far enough to suit Mohammad Mosaddeq's National Front, a multifaceted quasi-party that objected to foreign control of Iran's oil. Mosaddeq believed that Iran's oil revenues should be used to benefit the Iranian people, not to line the coffers of a foreign corporation. With this goal in mind, he launched successful campaigns to defeat the supplemental agreement and, after becoming prime minister, to nationalize the AIOC's Iranian holdings.[1]

The British reaction to these developments illustrated the concerns that would shape London's policy throughout the Iranian imbroglio. The AIOC's Iranian operations and its refinery at Abadan provided oil-starved Britain with twenty-two million tons of oil products and seven million tons of crude oil per year, including 85 percent of the fuel needed by the British Admiralty. They also generated £100 million in foreign exchange annually, which the British sorely needed during the financial crisis of 1951. Nor do these calculations tell the whole story. As Britain's largest overseas investment, the AIOC's Iranian operations stood as a symbol of British power in the Middle East. If those operations were nationalized, Great Britain's worldwide prestige, which was still reeling from the recent withdrawals from India and Palestine, would suffer and its vital assets elsewhere, such as the Suez Canal, would be jeopardized. Under these circumstances, the British were determined to do what they could to safeguard the AIOC's position in Iran and to resist what the Foreign Office called the «growing Near East practice of twisting the lion's tail.»[2]

---

1   For a general account of the Iranian oil crisis, from which much of the following story is taken, see Mary Ann Heiss, *Empire and Nationhood: The United States, Great Britain, and Iranian Oil, 1950–1954* (New York: Columbia University Press, 1997).
2   FO tel. 2103 to British Embassy, Washington, 18 May 1951, Foreign Office General Political Correspondence, Record Class FO 371, 91535/EP1531/354, Public Record Office, Kew, England.

Initially, the AIOC offered cosmetic and financial inducements that created the appearance but not the substance of Iranian control. When Mosaddeq rejected these inducements, they instituted a worldwide boycott of Iranian petroleum sales supported by the U.S. government and the major U.S. oil companies. By preventing Iran from reaping the benefits of nationalization, the boycott was designed to re-institute AIOC control of the oil industry. Although the boycott hurt Iran's economy, it did not lead to its collapse. Nor did it result in a more moderate oil posture. By the fall of 1951, the company had become convinced that its position in Iran was untenable. In a move described as Britain's «M[iddle] E[ast] Dunkirk» that generated «funeral headlines» in London, the AIOC withdrew from Iran and the country's oil exports ground to a halt. A year later, Iran severed diplomatic relations with Great Britain.[3]

If the British took an «empirical» approach to the Iranian oil dispute, U.S. policymakers emphasized the «higher» dangers involved.[4] As the only direct land barrier between the Soviet Union and the Persian Gulf, Iran served as a vital link in the Western alliance's Middle Eastern security chain; Soviet control of its territory would make the defense of Greece, Turkey, and the eastern Mediterranean all but impossible. Compounding Iran's importance were its rich oil resources, which U.S. policymakers considered crucial to the reconstruction and rearmament of Western Europe. Loss of these reserves would have dire consequences. In the short term, it would create serious shortages of aviation gasoline and other fuels needed for the military effort in Korea and raise the specter of civilian rationing. In the long term, it might compromise the West's ability to fight a protracted war with the Soviets, force augmentation of its military establishments, and result in an expansion of Soviet military bases in the Middle East. «Events in Iran,» warned U.S. officials in an articulation of the domino theory that would dominate their thinking during the Cold War, «cannot be separated from developments in such strategically vital nations as Egypt and Turkey.»[5] With so much resting on Iran's continued alliance with the West, the United States «could not take the chance of seeing [it] surrender to communism» or «fall into the Soviet orbit.»[6]

---

3 Walter S. Gifford (U.S. ambassador, London) tel. 1607 to State Department, 2 October 1951, General Records of the Department of State, Record Group 59, file: 888.2553/10 – 251, National Archives II, College Park, Maryland (hereafter RG 59, with filing information). For the British side of the Iranian nationalization crisis see Wm. Roger Louis, *The British Empire in the Middle East, 1945–1951: Arab Nationalism, the United States, and Postwar Imperialism* (Oxford: Oxford University Press, 1984), 632–89.

4 Sir Oliver Franks (British ambassador, Washington) tel. 427 to FO, 11 February 1952, FO 371, 98 685/EP15314/3l; Franks tel. 439 to FO, 12 February 1952, FO 371, 98 685/EP15314/32.

5 NSC-117, «The Anglo-Iranian Problem,» 10 October 1951, U.S. Department of State, *Foreign Relations of the United States, 1952–1954* (Washington: G.P.O., 1989), 10:220–22 (hereafter *FRUS*, with year and volume number).

6 Paper prepared in the Department of State, «The Present Crisis in Iran,» undated, *FRUS, 1950* (Washington, G.P.O., 1978), 5:505–19.

Initially, at least, American policymakers favored a negotiated Anglo-Iranian settlement that paid lip service to the idea of nationalization but also recognized Iran's contractual obligations to the AIOC. Such a settlement, they maintained, would preserve world peace and the global balance of power while still safeguarding both British and Iranian interests. Running throughout U.S. thinking during the early years of the crisis was the belief that British concessions held the key to a resolution. To prevent the loss of Iranian oil at a critical time for the Western alliance, U.S. officials advised the British to arrange some sort of partnership that did not involve «real [Iranian] equity ownership» but gave Tehran significant financial profits. Models of the sort of arrangement the U.S. government had in mind could be found in the relatively generous fifty-fifty profit-sharing deals the U.S. majors had negotiated with Venezuela and Saudi Arabia.[7] At the same time, U.S. officials urged Iranian moderation and cautioned against nationalization without compensation as well as abrogation of the company's concession against its will. In other words, Washington pressed consistently for a settlement that guaranteed both British and Iranian rights, and the Truman administration adopted a policy of benevolent neutrality that favored neither party in the dispute but advised caution and restraint on both.[8]

As the Iranian crisis dragged on, however, U.S. policymakers grew increasingly concerned about its potentially disastrous impact on Western security and came to believe that preserving British oil interests in Iran would go a long way toward defending Western interests there and throughout the Middle East. To this end, they decided to abandon their middle-of-the-road stance in Iran and to ally instead with traditional British interests. By the spring of 1952, U.S. officials had joined their British colleagues in decrying the chances of ever negotiating a settlement with Mosaddeq.[9] In late 1952, President Harry S. Truman joined Prime Minister Winston S. Churchill in a last-ditch effort at a compromise solution. Although this effort failed to resolve the Anglo-Iranian imbroglio, it signaled the culmination of Washington's transformation from an honest broker in the oil dispute to a full-fledged British partner and set the stage for closer Anglo-American cooperation in Iran.[10]

---

7   See Richard Funkhouser (Office of African and Near Eastern Affairs, State Department) memorandum for McGhee, «Summary – 11 September Meeting with Oil Officials,» 18 September 1950, in Senate Committee on Foreign Relations, Subcommittee on Multinational Corporations, *Multinational Corporations and United States Foreign Policy*, part 8, 93d Cong., 2d sess., 1974; and U.S. record of 10 April meeting between U.S. and U.K. delegations, 13 April 1951, FO 371, 91 471/EP1023/37.

8   For initial U.S. thinking see, for example, William Rountree (director, GTI [Office of Greek, Turkish, and Iranian Affairs, State Department]) memorandum of conversation, 18 April 1951, RG 59, 641.88/4 – 1851.

9   For the role of cultural factors in leading U.S. officials to this conclusion see Mary Ann Heiss, «Real Men Don't Wear Pajamas: Anglo-American Cultural Perceptions of Mohammed Mossadeq and the Iranian Oil Nationalization Dispute,» in *Empire and Revolution: The United States and the Third World since 1945*, ed. Peter L. Hahn and Mary Ann Heiss (Columbus: Ohio State University, 2001), 178–94.

10 See Loy W. Henderson (U.S. ambassador, Tehran) tel. to State Department, 25 August 1952, *FRUS, 1952–1954* 10:458–60; and David K. E. Bruce (State Department) tel. 481 to U.S. embassy, Tehran, 25 August 1952, RG 59, 888.2553/8–2552.

By the time Dwight D. Eisenhower took office in early 1953, the Iranian situation was approaching a crisis point. The Iranian government had negotiated a handful of oil sales deals with Italian and Japanese firms, but it had failed to break the British-led boycott by generating long-term sales contracts. Moreover, with world output now outstripping demand, extended contracts were unlikely, even though Iran was offering its oil at less than half the world price. In a move that caused serious concern among U.S. officials, it was even extending those prices to Soviet bloc states. Mosaddeq also fueled U.S. fears by entering into a tacit alliance with the Communist Tudeh party and by failing to stop mass public demonstrations that U.S. policymakers considered the prelude to full-scale social revolution. According to the shah, Mosaddeq was on course to become «the Dr. Benes of Iran.»[11] The Eisenhower administration agreed, and to keep Iran from going the way of Czechoslovakia, it decided to move against him. In August 1953, a coup supported by the British and American governments replaced Mosaddeq with Fazlollah Zahedi, who went on to negotiate an oil agreement that ensured continued Western domination of Iran's oil (including a 40 percent share for U.S. companies) and provided the economic foundation for the long rule of Mohammad Reza Shah. In October 1955, Iran joined the Baghdad Pact, and from that point until the Iranian Revolution in 1978, it served as the West's staunchest ally in the Middle East.[12]

Washington's concern with saving Iran from communism finally compelled it to abandon its efforts to work with Mosaddeq and to side with London instead. Preserving Iran's Western orientation and preventing Soviet control of its oil resources ultimately doomed all thought of a compromise settlement. In the end, Cold War considerations proved overriding. U.S. officials came to believe that the only way to protect Western interests in Iran was to support Britain's position and remove Mosaddeq, and their action ushered in twenty-five years of Iranian friendship with the West. But if the Iranian nationalization episode marked a triumph for Anglo-American cooperation, the bilateral differences that characterized its early stages served as a harbinger for the more serious transatlantic split that would come over Suez.

Only three years after Anglo-American cooperation helped to resolve the Iranian oil dispute, the crisis that began when Egyptian Prime Minister Gamal Abdel Nasser nationalized the Suez Canal tore the two allies apart. The British Foreign Office saw the conflict with Nasser as a reprise of the earlier struggle with Mosaddeq.[13] Like the battle for control of Ira-

---

11   Burton Y. Berry (U.S. ambassador, Baghdad) tel. to State Department, 17 August 1953, *FRUS, 1952–1954* 10:746–48. The effects of the British-led boycott may be followed in Mary Ann Heiss, «The International Boycott of Iranian and the Anti-Mosaddeq Coup of 1953,» in *Mohammed Mosaddeq and the 1953 Coup in Iran*, ed. Mark J. Gasiorowski and Malcolm Byrne (Syracuse: Syracuse University Press, 2004), 178–200.

12   For detailed examinations of the coup see the essays in Gasiorowski and Byrne, eds., *Mohammad Mosaddeq and the 1953 Coup in Iran*; and Stephen Kinzer, *All the Shah's Men: An American Coup and the Roots of Middle East Terror* (Hoboken: John Wiley & Sons, 2003).

nian oil, the fight over the Suez Canal threatened Britain's economic stability and worldwide prestige. Facing basically the same threat as in Iran, British officials adopted the same hardline attitude as well, even resorting to military action in concert with France and Israel to achieve their aims. Any other course, they feared, would be fatal to their position throughout the Middle East. U.S. officials disagreed. Convinced that military action would only drive Nasser into Moscow's arms, thereby endangering Western interests in the eastern Mediterranean and Middle East, they advised caution instead. Unlike the Iranian crisis, however, in which the Americans had abandoned moderation for a more pro-British stance as the crisis wore on, in the case of Suez there was no shift. Washington remained resolute in opposing a militant posture and ultimately forced London to reverse course.

The details of the Suez crisis have been well covered in the literature – including the work of several of our conference presenters – and only the barest outline is necessary here. After becoming prime minister in April 1954, Nasser negotiated an end to British military presence in the Suez Canal Zone, eschewed membership in the failed Middle East Command and Middle East Defense Organization and the North Atlantic Treaty Organization (NATO)-modeled Baghdad Pact, and laid plans for the construction of a hydroelectric dam at Aswan that would help to modernize the Egyptian economy. Although U.S. officials initially saw Nasser as a moderate nationalist with whom they could work and were quick to promise financial aid for the Aswan High Dam, his subsequent support for pan-Arabism and his cozying up to the Soviet bloc changed their minds. In July 1956, the Eisenhower administration withdrew its offer of aid for the Aswan Dam, whereupon Nasser nationalized the Suez Canal to make up the financial shortfall. Three months later, Britain, France, and Israel initiated a military operation designed to retake the canal, satisfy Israeli territorial designs, and remove Nasser from power.[14]

U.S. policymakers considered the operation a serious error; President Eisenhower called it «'the damnedest business [he] ever saw supposedly intelligent governments get themselves into.'» Nasser had a legal right to nationalize the canal, the Americans argued, so long as he compensated its former owners and kept it open to international traffic. Military intervention to retake it could lead to numerous difficulties. Egypt might retaliate by blocking Western access to the canal, a development that would not only have serious military implications for the Western position in the Middle East but also pose problems for Western European

---

13 For an account that links earlier developments in Egypt with the Iranian oil crisis see H. W. Brands, «The Cairo-Tehran Connection in Anglo-American Rivalry in the Middle East, 1951–1953,» *The International History Review* 11 (August 1989): 434–56.

14 For a general account of the Suez crisis see, for example, Peter L. Hahn, *The United States, Great Britain, and Egypt, 1945–1956: Strategy and Diplomacy in the Early Cold War* (Chapel Hill: University of North Carolina Press, 1991), 211–39; and Douglas Little, *American Orientalism: The United States and the Middle East since 1945* (Chapel Hill: University of North Carolina Press, 2004), 157–81. For an emphasis on oil diplomacy and alliance diplomacy see Ethan Kapstein, *The Insecure Alliance: Energy Crises ad Western Politics since 1944* (New York: Oxford University Press, 1990), 96–124.

oil consumers during the upcoming winter. Moreover, a military operation in Egypt would draw French and British troops away from NATO's European theater at a time of global tension. It was not clear, after all, whether the Soviet Union's recent intervention in Hungary was to be a jumping-off point for a larger assault. Beyond these tangible dangers, intervention carried intangible ones as well. It would inflame anti-Western sentiment in the Arab world, push Nasser deeper into the Soviet camp, and allow Moscow to step in as the defender of small nations against Western imperialism. According to Eisenhower, military action «'might well array the world from Dakar to the Philippine Islands against us'» and generate hostility that «'could not be overcome in a generation and, perhaps, not even in a century.'»[15]

When asked to sanction the intervention beforehand, U.S. officials had demurred. After the allies struck anyway, they condemned the operation that made it impossible for the West to launch a propaganda attack against concurrent Soviet heavy-handedness in Hungary and worked through the United Nations to arrange a cease-fire. When Anglo-French troops were slow to withdraw, Washington resorted to economic and financial – particularly oil – sanctions to speed things along. The power of such sanctions stemmed from the fact that by the winter of 1956–57, Britain and France were facing a severe shortage of oil. Nasser had blocked the Suez Canal during the initial days of the confrontation, saboteurs had cut the oil pipelines across Syria, and Saudi Arabia had halted oil sales to Britain and France. Only oil from the United States could make up the shortfall, but Eisenhower refused to make that oil available until the allies had pulled out of Suez. For the administration, in a development whose importance cannot be overestimated, oil was to become a tool of U.S. diplomacy. British officials themselves were well aware of the effect that sanctions would have on their Suez operation; upon learning of Washington's intentions, Chancellor of the Exchequer Harold Macmillan famously exclaimed, «'Oil sanctions! That finishes it.'»[16]

As in the Iranian crisis, Anglo-American differences over Suez revealed the array of fears and concerns that motivated officials in London and Washington. Policymakers in the Foreign Office were again concerned about Britain's global position and sought to preserve at least a modicum of its former influence in Egypt. They saw the battle over Suez as part of the struggle between the developed and developing worlds, between what world systems scholars call the core and the periphery. As the core nation responsible for Egypt and the rest of the Middle East under the postwar Anglo-American division of labor, Britain alone should determine how to protect what it saw as the Western core's interests in that region. And for officials in London, those interests could best be protected by a firm stand at Suez, even if that stand risked war. Giving in to Nasser, they maintained, would lead to the complete expulsion of «'all Western influence and interests from [the] Arab countries'» and else-

---

15 Eisenhower quoted in Hahn, *Strategy and Diplomacy*, 232, 215, 218.
16 Macmillan quoted in Yergin, *The Prize*, 492. For the importance of U.S. oil sanctions see Diane B. Kunz, *The Economic Diplomacy of the Suez Crisis* (Chapel Hill: University of North Carolina Press, 1991).

where.[17] Closer to home, and perhaps more to the point, Harold Macmillan feared that it would turn Britain into «'another Netherlands.'».[18]

U.S. officials agreed that Suez was part of the global struggle between the developed and developing worlds. But for them the real danger lay not in a victory for the forces of nationalism but in the triumph of communism. As policymakers in the State Department saw things, British bellicosity would only confirm Egyptian impressions of Western imperialism, steel Nasser's determination to rid his nation of Western influence, and cement his ties with the Soviet Union. It might also lead to an Arab embargo of oil sales to the Western nations, a development that would have serious economic and strategic implications, or to a complete Soviet takeover of the Middle East, which would completely reconfigure the East-West balance of power.[19]

For the United States, the goal of preventing the spread of communism dictated the adoption in Egypt of the opposite strategy from the one pursued in Iran. There the need to stop a possible Soviet advance had led Washington to subordinate the needs of Iranian nationalism to traditional British interests: Containment in Iran could best be accomplished by propping up the British position and using London as the bulwark of Western power. In Egypt, the situation was reversed. Now it was the British position that had to be subordinated, even at the risk of undermining Britain's global position and precipitating a transatlantic split. During the three years that separated the Iranian and Suez disputes, U.S. officials had concluded that they could no longer hope to contain Soviet influence in the Middle East by backing the British and crushing indigenous nationalism. On the contrary, such a strategy would only inflame nationalist sentiment, threaten to tar the United States with the brush of British imperialism, and make a Soviet takeover of the region all the more likely. This did not mean that U.S. officials shared Nasser's goals. It simply meant that mollifying Egyptian nationalism became the preferred U.S. tactic for achieving the goal of containment. The overriding anti-Communist orientation of U.S. policy remained constant. What had changed, as Peter Hahn has noted, was that the United States now had to choose between two interests that previously had coincided: support for the British and containment of the Soviets. Given contemporary Cold War tensions, the choice was a foregone conclusion.[20]

In many respects, the Suez crisis was a turning point in the postwar history of Eastern and Western relations with Egypt and the Middle East. For the East, the crisis initiated a new spirit of amity between Moscow and Cairo; by the 1960s, the Soviets counted Nasser as one of their closest allies in the Middle East and, in fact, in all of the developing world.[21] For the West, the crisis had less auspicious results. It marked the last gasp of British imperialism in

---

17   Eden quoted in Kapstein, *Insecure Alliance*, 112.
18   Macmillan quoted in Brian Lapping, *End of Empire* (New York: St. Martin's Press, 1985), 266.
19   See William Stivers, «Eisenhower and the Middle East,» in *Reevaluating Eisenhower: American Foreign Policy in the 1950s*, ed. Richard A. Melanson and David Mayers (Urbana: University of Illinois Press, 1987), 192–219.
20   See Hahn, *Strategy and Diplomacy*, 238.

the Middle East and, much like France's defeat at Dien Bien Phu thirty months earlier, served as painful confirmation that Britain was no longer a great power.[22] It also caused a serious rift in the Anglo-American alliance and engendered British and French animosity toward the United States that was soon papered over but not entirely ameliorated.[23] Finally, the Suez crisis pushed the United States to play a greater role in trying to stabilize the Middle East and hold the line against Communist expansion or potentially destabilizing indigenous nationalism there. The Eisenhower Doctrine authorizing the use of U.S. armed forces to defend U.S.-friendly regimes in the region against overt «armed aggression from any nation controlled by International Communism» codified this new policy in January 1957.[24] U.S. aid to Jordan later that year and intervention in the Lebanese civil war in 1958 put it into practice.[25] The decades after the Suez crisis would see a sharpening of all of these trends, as Middle Eastern events – particularly the escalating Arab-Israeli conflict and the consequences of the West's growing dependence on imported oil – exacerbated existing U.S.-European differences and ultimately reshaped the Western alliance.

The relative calm that characterized the Arab-Israeli conflict during the decade following the Suez crisis was shattered in June 1967, when Israel locked horns with Egypt, Syria, and Jordan during the Six-Day War. Although American support for Israel and Soviet support for the Arabs was widely known, neither superpower overtly intervened in the conflict, and Israel secured a tremendous military victory on its own, capturing control of the Sinai, the West Bank of the Jordan, the Golan Heights, and East Jerusalem. If the superpowers largely refrained from influencing the course of the war, however, both used the conflict to enhance their own positions in the Middle East, with the United States cementing its ties with Israel and the Soviet Union strengthening its links with the Arab states. The short-lived June War also affected the Western allies. French President Charles de Gaulle, who in 1966 had withdrawn France from NATO's integrated military command, further split with his Western allies by condemning Israel for firing the conflict's first shot and by halting French arms sales to Tel Aviv. These developments signaled de Gaulle's determination to pursue a more independent course in international affairs and opened the door for the significant American

---

21 See William B. Quandt, «U.S.-Soviet Rivalry in the Middle East,» in *East-West Tensions in the Third World*, ed. Marshall D. Shulman and William H. Sullivan (New York: W. W. Norton, 1986), 32.

22 The connection between Suez and Dien Bien Phu is made in Scott L. Bills, «The United States, NATO, and the Third World: Dominoes, Imbroglios, and Agonizing Reappraisals,» in *NATO after Forty Years*, ed. Lawrence S. Kaplan et al. (Wilmington: Scholarly Resources Inc., 1990), 160.

23 For Anglo-American relations in the Middle East after Suez see Stephen J. Blackwell, «A Transfer of Power? Britain, the Anglo-American Relationship and the Cold War in the Middle East, 1957–1962,» in *Cold War Britain, 1945–1964: New Perspectives*, ed. Michael F. Hopkins, Michael D. Kandiah, and Gillian Staerck (New York: Palgrave Macmillan, 2003), 168–79.

24 «Joint Congressional Resolution to Promote Peace and Stability in the Middle East,» 9 March 1957, U.S. Department of State, *United States Policy in the Middle East, September 1956-June 1957* (Washington: G.P.O., 1957), 44–46.

25 On Lebanon see Douglas Little, «His Finest Hour? Eisenhower, Lebanon, and the 1958 Middle East Crisis,» in Hahn and Heiss, eds., *Empire and Revolution*, 17–47.

arms sales to Israel that would characterize the post-1967 period. They also portended the more serious cracks in the Western alliance that would appear during the 1973 Yom Kippur War.

The Arab oil embargo that accompanied the October 1973 war exacerbated the problems within the Western alliance that had characterized the Six-Day War. For the Western Europeans, who received two-thirds of their oil from Arab countries, the embargo threatened their energy security and economic well being. But instead of confronting it together, they worked individually to protect their own supplies, even to the point of undercutting each other with the Arabs in order to secure oil. For U.S. officials, the embargo was an effort to blackmail them into abandoning Israel and allowing the Soviet-backed Arabs to control the Middle East. To prevent such an outcome, they tried to effect a diplomatic solution to the Yom Kippur War that gave each side some, but not all, of what it wanted and prevented the superpowers from intervening on behalf of their respective regional clients. They also tried to forge a common consumer response to the embargo that would negate its divisive effects for the Western allies and defuse its usefulness as a political weapon. Although the United States was able to keep the Yom Kippur War from becoming a superpower conflict, it was less successful on the oil front. By the time the embargo ended, the Western alliance's oil security policy lay in tatters, as did the solidarity that had constituted its cornerstone.

Ostensibly, the oil embargo was aimed at weakening U.S. support for Israel. In the years since the Six-Day War, and especially since the 1970 Jordanian crisis, Washington had provided Israel with extensive military aid – $1.2 billion in credits in 1972 and 1973 alone. It had also tacitly supported Israeli occupation of territories seized in 1967, namely, the Sinai, the West Bank, the Golan Heights, and East Jerusalem.[26] Israel's occupation of these areas was anathema to all of the Arab states, but none more than Egypt, which was determined to avenge its humiliating 1967 defeat at all costs. Hence President Anwar Sadat's decision for a joint Egyptian-Syrian attack in October 1973.[27] To provide for a united Arab front in the conflict and to press the West into abandoning Israel, Sadat had convinced Saudi Arabia's King Faisal to institute an embargo. As the Arab world's largest oil producer, Saudi Arabia was the key to an embargo's success. Although Faisal initially resisted the idea, preferring instead to lead a (successful) campaign for higher oil prices on world markets, visible U.S. support for Israel during the Yom Kippur War changed his mind.[28]

---

26 See, for example, William B. Quandt, *Decade of Decisions: American Policy toward the Arab-Israeli Conflict, 1967–1976* (Berkeley: University of California Press, 1977), 65–68, 105–27; and Steven L. Spiegel, *The Other Arab-Israeli Conflict: Making America's Middle East Policy, from Truman to Reagan* (Chicago: University of Chicago Press, 1985), 158–65.

27 For an Arab perspective on this period see Mohamed Heikal, *The Road to Ramadan* (New York: Quadrangle, 1975).

28 For Arab thinking regarding the oil embargo see George Lenczowski, «The Oil-Producing Countries,» in *The Oil Crisis*, ed. Raymond Vernon (New York: W. W. Norton, 1976), 59–72.

From its beginning the embargo strained relations among the Western nations, which the Arabs divided into three categories based on their support for Israel. The United States and the Netherlands, considered Israel's biggest supporters, would be completely cut off from Arab oil; Britain and France, seen as «friendly» to Arab interests, would receive the same amount of Arab oil as in the past; and the other European NATO partners (along with Japan), strong supporters of neither side, would see their oil imports decline monthly until the Yom Kippur War was settled. But those countries that would continue to receive Arab oil would pay significantly higher prices: During the last three months of 1973 alone, the posted price of Middle Eastern crude doubled, from $5.12 per barrel to $11.65.[29]

To deal with the embargo, the major oil companies adopted an «equal suffering» policy under which all countries would endure the same percentage decrease in normal oil supplies regardless of their status on the Arab list. For the companies, this was the only «equitable and practical» course of action: It ensured that no nation received better treatment than any other and safeguarded the integrity of their international contracts.[30] For the Western Europeans, however, and especially for the French and the British, it was an unfair policy that penalized them in favor of the pro-Israeli Americans.[31]

When it proved impossible to alter the companies' policy, the Western Europeans decided to curry favor with the Arabs instead. On 6 November 1973, they called upon Israel to accept UN Resolution 242, by which the Arabs would recognize Israel's right to exist in exchange for Israeli withdrawal from territories seized during the 1967 war. This move had the desired effect, as the Arabs subsequently exempted the European nations (except the Netherlands) from future production cuts. But Western Europe's united front was temporary. After a December summit meeting in Copenhagen failed to yield a common voice regarding the oil crisis, the European nations began separate bilateral negotiations with various producing countries designed to swap industrial goods and technological aid for oil. In a clear violation of both the letter and the spirit of community regulations, they also refused to ship oil to the embargoed Dutch, beginning such shipments only after the Dutch threatened to withhold natural gas from Belgium, France, and West Germany if they did not receive oil assistance from their allies.[32] By early 1974, the Arab oil producers had shrewdly

---

29 See Yergin, *The Prize*, 625.
30 Royal Dutch/Shell executive Geoffrey Chandler quoted in Robert J. Lieber, *Oil and the Middle East War: Europe in the Energy Crisis* (Cambridge: Center for International Affairs, Harvard University, 1976), 16. For more on company efforts to handle the oil crisis see Yergin, *The Prize*, 619–22; and Robert B. Stobaugh, «The Oil Companies in the Crisis,» in Vernon, ed., *The Oil Crisis*, 179–202.
31 See Yergin, *The Prize*, 623–24; and Frank R. Wyant, *The United States, OPEC, and Multinational Oil* (Lexington: D. C. Heath, 1977), 131–32.
32 For the European response to the Arab oil embargo see, for example, Kapstein, *Insecure Alliance*, 166–68; Yergin, *The Prize*, 626–29; and Wolfgang Hager, «Western Europe: The Politics of Muddling Through,» and Hans Maull, «The Strategy of Avoidance: Europe's Middle East Policies after the October War,» in *Oil, the Arab-Israeli Dispute, and the Industrial World: Horizons of Crisis*, ed. J. C. Hurewitz (Boulder: Westview Press, 1976), 34–51, 110–37.

divided the Atlantic Alliance, pitting the Western Europeans against both the Americans and each other.

The French and the British were the most vehement about distancing themselves from the Americans and pursuing independent approaches to the Arabs. Partly this was a practical matter: As French President Georges Pompidou noted, while the United States received only 10 percent of its oil from Arab countries and could afford to alienate them by supporting Israel, France was «entirely dependent» on Arab oil and hardly in a position to do likewise. It is also probable that the French and the British saw opposition to U.S. policy as a way of avenging what they saw as earlier U.S. betrayals elsewhere. The French, for example, had never quite forgiven officials in Washington for scotching their plans to employ NATO forces in the war against Algerian rebels.[33] And the British, as Daniel Yergin has pointed out, saw opposition to the United States as payback for what they considered the U.S. betrayal at Suez. Although British Prime Minister Edward Heath denied personally that he «'wanted to raise the issue of Suez,'» he admitted that it was «'there for many people.'»[34]

Europe's oil-driven mentality displeased U.S. officials, who viewed the events of 1973 within a Cold War context. For them, the Yom Kippur War and the oil embargo were more than manifestations of the Arab-Israeli conflict; they were also components of the ongoing struggle between communism and capitalism. The Arab states, especially Egypt and Syria, received extensive arms support from the Soviet Union, and their victory in the Yom Kippur War would allow the Soviets to dominate the entire Middle East. To prevent such an eventuality, the West, led by the United States, had to assist Israel, even if doing so angered the Arabs and contributed to the oil embargo. But it also had to prevent the kind of humiliating Arab defeat that might invite Soviet intervention and thereby transform the Yom Kippur War into World War III. To this end, Secretary of State Henry Kissinger undertook a frenzied campaign of shuttle diplomacy that finally resulted in a cease-fire on 25 October.[35]

No thanks to the European NATO nations, though, which did not share Washington's geopolitical view of the 1973 crisis and which wanted nothing to do with a possible superpower disengagement in the Middle East. To avoid becoming embroiled in a Soviet-American confrontation, the Western European NATO partners generally refused to support U.S. efforts to re-supply Israel during the October war. Aside from the Netherlands, only Portugal granted landing rights to U.S. planes carrying supplies to Israel, an act that earned it Arab enmity and got it added to the list of countries completely cut off from Arab oil. France continued throughout the conflict to ship tanks to Libya and Saudi Arabia; Turkey even allowed Soviet planes carrying supplies to Egypt and Syria to violate its airspace without protest.[36]

33 See Gillian Staerck, «The Algerian War, De Gaulle, and Anglo-American Relations, 1958,» in Hopkins, Kandiah, and Staerck, eds., *Cold War Britain*,155–67.
34 Pompidou and Heath quoted in Yergin, *The Prize*, 627–28.
35 On the U.S. diplomatic efforts to end the Yom Kippur War see Alan Dowty, *Middle East Crisis: U.S. Decision-Making in 1958, 1970, and 1979* (Berkeley: University of California Press, 1984), 199–277.
36 See Kapstein, *Insecure Alliance*, 165; and Lieber, *Oil and the Middle East War*, 12.

The Western Europeans also made it clear that they would block any U.S. attempt to use NATO facilities against the Soviets in the Middle East. Their proximity to Soviet missiles in Eastern Europe and their fears of a Soviet attack overrode their sense of alliance solidarity, prompting Kissinger to lament that they were acting «'as if the [Atlantic] alliance did not exist.'»[37]

American-European differences were also evident in the handling of the embargo. To Washington's way of thinking, the Arabs had made the oil weapon work by subordinating their individual differences to a common goal. Successfully resisting the embargo required the consuming nations to do the same rather than adopting a *sauve qui peut* («every man for himself») approach and cutting their own deals with the Arabs at the expense of their allies. Such action only played into the Arabs' hands, allowed them to raise oil prices dramatically, and weakened the Western position in the Middle East and throughout the world. It also threatened to ally Western Europe more closely with the Arab cause, a development that would seriously complicate U.S. efforts to achieve a permanent Arab-Israeli settlement.[38] Given the differences over the Yom Kippur War and the oil embargo, 1973 hardly turned out to be the «Year of Europe» that Nixon and Kissinger had envisioned.

The disjointed Western response to the oil embargo was finally resolved in February 1974, when the NATO nations and Japan convened, under U.S. auspices, for the Washington Energy Conference. Coming as it did on the heels of the scramble for Arab oil, the conference was, in Kissinger's words, more like «a clash of adversaries» than «a meeting of allies.»[39] Tensions were indeed high as the participants advanced different solutions to the oil problem. Britain and France, for example, called for a distinctly European energy policy, while West Germany backed an American plan for consumer unity.[40] The deadlock was only broken when President Richard M. Nixon issued a veiled threat to pull U.S. troops out of Europe unless the NATO allies abandoned their intransigence on oil.[41] Ultimately unwilling to compromise their overall security by breaking with the Americans on energy, the Western Europeans agreed to join the U.S.-sponsored International Energy Agency, a supranational organization designed to provide the kind of concerted policy that had been sorely lacking during the 1973–74 Arab embargo. In keeping with its past efforts at greater independence from the United States and the Western alliance, France declined to join.[42]

---

37 Walter Laquer, *Confrontation: The Middle East and World Politics* (New York: Quadrangle, 1974), 207.
38 See Yergin, *The Prize*, 629; and Lieber, *Oil and the Middle East War*, 20.
39 Henry Kissinger, *Years of Upheaval* (Boston: Little Brown, 1982), 905.
40 See Kapstein, *Insecure Alliance*, 171–75; and Yergin, *The Prize*, 629–30.
41 See Kissinger, *Years of Upheaval*, 916.
42 For the International Energy Agency see Kapstein, *Insecure Alliance*, chap. 8; and Wilfrid L. Kohl, «The International Energy Agency: The Political Context,» in Hurewitz, ed., *Oil, the Arab-Israeli Dispute, and the Industrial World*, 246–57.

The 1973 embargo had far-reaching ramifications. It marked the first successful Arab use of the oil weapon and indicated that in the future, producer countries would not hesitate to use their new economic power to achieve their political goals. The embargo also effected a significant redistribution of wealth from the developed West to the developing Middle East and allowed the Arab oil exporters to emerge (at least for a time) as philanthropists to the least developed nations of the world.[43] For the NATO countries, the embargo revealed the fragile sense of community that bound them together and the ease with which autarkic self-interest could tear them apart. It also marked the apogee of Soviet influence in the Arab world and ushered in a period of improving relations between the United States and key Arab states like Egypt and Saudi Arabia.

The period after 1974 witnessed a significant increase in the U.S. presence in the Middle East, as Washington assumed primary responsibility for protecting Western interests in the region. Although U.S. policymakers continued to worry about the possible expansion of Soviet influence in the region, they also became more concerned than previously about the potentially destabilizing effects of indigenous Middle Eastern nationalism and intra-regional disputes. Both of these threats could plunge the Middle East into armed conflict and imperil vital Western petroleum and security interests. To protect those interests, the United States augmented its regional presence and demonstrated its resolve to use force in defense of its Middle East position, even if doing so meant acting without its European allies.

Immediately following the Yom Kippur War, the United States emerged as the driving force behind an Arab-Israeli settlement. Years of painstaking diplomacy finally yielded the historic 1978 Camp David Accords and the 1979 Egyptian-Israeli peace treaty, which greatly reduced the chances of another Arab-Israeli war and went a long way toward stabilizing the entire Middle East.[44] Yet acclaim for the Egyptian-Israeli treaty was not universal. The other Arab states denounced Egypt for selling out to Israel, but because Egypt was the key to any viable Arab bloc, their opposition was in the end ineffectual. The Western Europeans were also critical, largely because the treaty made no provision for settling the Palestinian question; in June 1980 they issued their own, more pro-Palestinian policy statement, the Venice Declaration.[45] But if European opposition prevented a united Western front regarding the Arab-Israeli dispute and served as a harbinger of future obstacles to a permanent peace, it did not derail progress toward a settlement. By the late 1970s, the United States had clearly emerged as the dominant Western power in brokering an end to the long-simmering Arab-Israeli dispute. When Jimmy Carter left the White House in 1981, that conflict, while not

---

43 For this development see Zuhayr Mikdashi, «The OPEC Process,» in Vernon, ed., *The Oil Crisis*, 211.
44 See Spiegel, *Other Arab-Israeli Conflict*, chaps. 7 and 8.
45 For the Palestinian question see Janice Gross Stein, «Alice in Wonderland: The North Atlantic Alliance and the Arab-Israeli Dispute,» in *The Middle East and the Western Alliance*, ed. Steven L. Spiegel (London: George Allen & Unwin, 1982), 60–72; for the European position see Raymond Cohen, «Twice Bitten? The European Community's 1987 Middle East Initiative,» *Middle East Review* 20 (Spring 1988): 33–40.

permanently resolved, appeared to be receding as a major source of Middle Eastern instability.

This did not mean that all was well in the region. On the contrary, just as Arab-Israeli tensions were ebbing, the Iranian Revolution and the Soviet invasion of Afghanistan destabilized the Western position there. The 1978 Islamic Revolution in Iran, which transformed the West's staunchest Middle Eastern ally into a hostile, anti-Western state, was seen as a gain for Moscow because it was a loss for Washington. The result of long-simmering domestic opposition to the abuses of Mohammed Reza Shah's reign, the Islamic Revolution rekindled U.S. fears of regional nationalism – now with a fundamentalist twist.[46] The almost concurrent invasion of Afghanistan, which bordered Iran, was even more threatening. It conjured up U.S. fears of a Soviet master plan to gain access to a warm water port and oil reserves in the Persian Gulf, possibly by capitalizing on the turmoil surrounding the Iranian Revolution. It also altered the East-West balance in the region by placing Soviet troops within striking distance of vital Middle Eastern oilfields and important NATO military bases.[47]

Both of these developments refocused Western interests on the importance of developments in the Middle East, though neither yielded a truly unified response.[48] Officials in Washington saw the Iranian and Afghani incidents from a global perspective and called for a common Western front. After Iranian militants seized the U.S. embassy in Tehran in November 1979, Washington pressed its European allies to apply economic sanctions against Tehran and to reduce the size of their embassy staffs there. Similar calls for united action, ranging from boycotting the 1980 Olympic Games in Moscow to military support for anti-Soviet rebels, followed the invasion of Afghanistan. But these pleas went unheeded, as the European NATO allies continued to emphasize local concerns over global ones and to believe that the U.S. government over-exaggerated the threats inherent in the Iranian and Afghani crises. For the Europeans, the overriding goals in the Middle East remained preventing another oil shortage and avoiding conflict with Moscow, and those goals could best be attained by a neutral response to the problems in Iran and Afghanistan.[49]

---

46 For Iran see, for example, James A. Bill, *The Eagle and the Lion: The Tragedy of American-Iranian Relations* (New Haven: Yale University Press, 1988), 216–60.

47 For concerns about Afghanistan see Gianni Bonvinici, «Out-of-Area Issues: A New Challenge to the Atlantic Alliance,» in *The Atlantic Alliance and the Middle East*, ed. Joseph I. Coffey and Gianni Bonvinici (Pittsburgh: University of Pittsburgh Press, 1989), 2; and Dominique Moisi, «Europe and the Middle East,» in Spiegel, ed., *The Middle East and the Western Alliance*, 31.

48 See, for example, The Atlantic Council of the United States, Working Group on Security Affairs, *After Afghanistan – The Long Haul: Safeguarding Security and Independence in the Third World* (Boulder: Westview Press, 1980); and Lawrence S. Kaplan, «The United States, NATO, and the Third World: Security Issues in Historical Perspective,» in *East-West Rivalry in the Third World: Security Issues and Regional Perspectives*, ed. Robert W. Clawson (Wilmington: Scholarly Resources Inc., 1986), 3.

49 See Lincoln P. Bloomfield, «Crisis Management outside the NATO Area: Allies of Competitors?» and S. I. P. van Campen, «NATO Political Consultation and European Political Cooperation,» in *Allies in a Turbulent World: Challenges to U.S. and Western European Cooperation*, ed. Frans A. M. Alting von Geusau (Lexington: D. C. Heath, 1982), 53, 70–71.

In a fashion that was becoming increasingly common, after 1980 the United States acted unilaterally to meet what it saw as new challenges in the Persian Gulf. In the Carter Doctrine, issued in January 1980, Washington indicated its intention to defend its Persian Gulf interests from outside threats – that is, Soviet aggression – by any means necessary, even a resort to force. «A successful take-over of Afghanistan,» Carter later recalled, «would give the Soviets a deep penetration between Iran and Pakistan and pose a threat to the rich oil fields of the Persian Gulf area.» To back up this new policy, the Carter administration began and the Reagan administration completed plans to upgrade U.S. capabilities for dealing with threats in what Washington now called Southwest Asia. In 1983, these plans resulted in the U.S. Central Command (CENTCOM), a rapid-response force that could quickly address regional tensions.[50] Other episodes throughout the 1980s reflected Washington's growing tendency to act unilaterally in the Middle East and its determination to protect what it saw as important U.S. interests in the region. For example, the United States took the lead in trying to stabilize Lebanon, where rival Christians, Muslims, and Palestinians had been locked in civil war since 1975. Over time, both Syria and Israel had sent troops to Lebanon – Syria because it wanted to prevent a victory by radical Muslims and Palestinians, Israel because it wanted to stop Palestinian guerrilla attacks coming from southern Lebanon. Ostensibly to stabilize the situation and allow the Lebanese government to reestablish order but ultimately for their own individual reasons, the United States, France, and Italy joined in a multinational force in Lebanon. Although the initial task was completed rather easily, permanent peace was more elusive, and the United States seemed on the brink of being dragged into a Vietnam-style quagmire. The October 1983 suicide bombing of U.S. Marine headquarters in Beirut that killed almost 250 Americans eliminated the threat of a protracted American presence in Lebanon and convinced the Reagan administration to reverse course. In early 1984, Washington announced that the marines were being moved to a more defensible position. Lebanon had not been stabilized, and the intervention ultimately proved fruitless.[51]

The United States also arrogated to itself responsibility for neutralizing Libya's Muammar Qaddafi, who by the mid-1980s had become its latest Middle Eastern bête noire. After assuming power in 1969, Qaddafi had nationalized Western oil interests in Libya and launched a concerted attack against Western interests in general, to the point of condoning and in fact supporting international terrorism. In April 1986, in retaliation for what was thought to have been the Libyan-backed bombing of a nightclub in West Berlin that killed two U.S. soldiers and injured scores of others, U.S. bombers struck Libyan targets at will, killing many but failing either to dislodge Qaddafi from power or to deter him from sup-

---

50 Jimmy Carter, *Keeping Faith: Memoirs of a President* (New York: Bantam, 1982), 471–72. See Jed C. Snyder, *Defending the Fringe: NATO, the Mediterranean, and the Persian Gulf* (Boulder: Westview Press, 1987), 116–19.
51 See Maya Chedda, *Paradox of Power: The United States in Southwest Asia, 1973–1984* (Santa Barbara: ABC-Clio, 1986), 153–73.

porting anti-American terrorism. Moreover, American heavy-handedness in dealing with Qaddafi elicited strong opposition from the European NATO partners, who advocated a political rather than a military settlement of U.S.-Libyan differences. France and Spain were especially outspoken against U.S. intervention, refusing over flight rights to U.S. bombers headed for Libya.[52] All things considered, the unilateral American interventions in Lebanon and Libya failed to accomplish their main goals. But they did indicate how determined the United States had become to protect its Middle Eastern interests from perceived threats, even if it had to act without its allies to do so.

Concurrent with these instances of Western squabbling regarding the Middle East was the 1980–1988 Iran-Iraq War, which evinced cooperation but not concerted alliance action. The war stemmed from a long-standing border dispute rather than from outside (that is, Soviet) pressures and evolved for the most part without much third-party intervention. To be sure, U.S. policymakers, and their counterparts in Western Europe, feared that an Iranian victory would mean the spread of Islamic fundamentalism throughout the Gulf region and threaten Western petroleum and security interests in Saudi Arabia and elsewhere. But aside from France, which openly aided Iraq in the conflict, Western nations refrained from supporting either side and sought instead to stay out of what became an increasingly bloody and brutal stalemate.[53] They did, though, take an active interest in keeping the conflict from spreading and in protecting the continued flow of oil through the Persian Gulf. To this end, early on in the war, the United States, along with Britain and France, had sent warships to the Gulf region not only in a show of force but also to escort foreign-owned oil tankers. The allies expanded their efforts after the Iranians began attacking Kuwaiti oil tankers in the Persian Gulf in the summer of 1986. These attacks could seriously threaten the United States and Western Europe, which received 15 and 46 percent of their oil, respectively, from the Persian Gulf. They could also provide an opportunity for an expansion of Soviet influence in the region if Moscow decided to assist Kuwait in protecting its tankers. To thus avert what officials in Washington considered a double-sided danger, the United States agreed to re-flag Kuwaiti tankers under the Stars and Stripes and to provide those tankers with naval escorts through the Gulf. The major Western allies, including France, Great Britain, Italy, Belgium, and the Netherlands, added their own naval vessels to the transport effort and thereby helped to effect an independent but coordinated response to what all could agree was a serious threat to their common petroleum interests in the Middle East.[54]

The driving force behind the concerted Western response to the Iran-Iraq War was clearly the United States. Washington's de facto involvement in that conflict served to con-

---

52 See Maurizio Cremasco, «Do-it-Yourself: National Approaches to the Out-of-Area Question,» in Coffey and Bonvinici, eds., *The Atlantic Alliance and the Middle East*, 180–85; and Snyder, *Defending the Fringe*, 113–16.
53 For French policy see Cremasco, «Do-it-Yourself,» 159.
54 See Michael A. Palmer, *Guardians of the Gulf: A History of America's Expanding Role in the Persian Gulf, 1833–1992* (New York: Free Press, 1992), 108–9, 118–27.

firm its determination to protect Persian Gulf stability from all perceived challenges, be they external or internal. With the Soviet Union of the Gorbachev era becoming less of a threat to Western interests in the Middle East, U.S. policymakers now came to appreciate the real danger posed by indigenous regional tensions and began formulating a strategy for dealing with them. They increased the U.S. military presence in the Gulf; strengthened their ties to relatively moderate Middle Eastern states like Kuwait and Saudi Arabia; and even sought to improve their relations with Iraq, which they saw as less of a threat to Western regional interests than Iran.[55] As later developments made clear, however, that assumption was dangerously inaccurate.

Iraq's August 1990 assault against Kuwait elicited the same determination to protect U.S. interests in the Persian Gulf as previous regional crises. It also provided still another opportunity for alliance cooperation. The international community, including the United States, its NATO allies, and the Soviet Union, was quick to condemn the Iraqi invasion. Over thirty nations also eventually joined the U.S.-led coalition that pulled off Operation Desert Shield/Desert Storm and forced Iraq out of Kuwait. The Gulf War solidified the position of the United States as the primary Western power working for stability in the Persian Gulf and protecting smaller, oil-rich Gulf states like Kuwait and Saudi Arabia from outside attack, even after the end of the Cold War had removed the specter of Soviet expansion from the horizon.[56]

Developments since the Persian Gulf War confirmed the growing U.S. determination to stabilize the Middle East and to shape regional developments according to Washington's own worldview. The administration of George H. W. Bush decided not to carry the Gulf War to Baghdad and allowed Saddam Hussein to remain in power. It did work through the United Nations, though, to curtail his various weapons programs through economic sanctions and international inspections. Saddam chafed under these restrictions but remained a thorn in the side of Bush's successor, William Jefferson Clinton. The Clinton administration devoted the lion's share of its Middle Eastern attention not to Iraq, however, but to the hoary Arab-Israeli problem. As Douglas Little has pointed out, the administration's efforts in this respect – like those of so many of its predecessors – amounted to little more than «a fool's errand to the Holy Land.»[57] Clinton's successor, George W. Bush, returned the focus of U.S. Middle East policy to Iraq, particularly after the 9/11 terrorist attacks. Despite the lack of credible evidence linking Iraq to Osama bin Laden's terrorist network, the administration launched a military campaign in Iraq in March 2003. Saddam was quickly removed from power, but the long-term stabilization of Iraq has proven more difficult. Justification for the move

---

55 See ibid., 150–62; and H. W. Brands, *Into the Labyrinth: The United States and the Middle East, 1945–1993* (New York: McGraw-Hill, 1994), 192–96.
56 See Phebe Marr, «The Persian Gulf after the Storm,» in *Riding the Tiger: The Middle East Challenge after the Cold War*, ed. Phebe Marr and William Lewis (Boulder: Westview Press, 1993), 109–35.
57 Little, *American Orientalism*, 314.

against Saddam was laid out beforehand in the administration's September 2002 «National Security Strategy of the United States of America,» a starkly – almost apocalyptically – written blueprint for U.S. foreign policy.[58] The NSS moved well beyond any of the nation's Cold War-era foreign policy pronouncements and removed any shred of doubt about Washington's determination to bend the world to fit the needs and interests of the United States. Although the NSS paid lip service to the need for consultation with allies, such calls could not hide what was essentially a claim for U.S. unilateralism. The ultimate aim, in fact, seemed nothing less than complete U.S. hegemony – in the Middle East and beyond.

The six decades since World War II have witnessed the growing involvement of the United States in the Middle East, an involvement motivated by a multiplicity of factors. Protecting U.S. – and Western – access to the region's oil supplies has been a constant goal. So has ensuring that strategic pieces of regional real estate remain out of the hands of hostile forces, whether the Soviet Union, regional nationalists, or other untrustworthy elements. Another constant theme for U.S. postwar policy in the Middle East has been the effect of regional developments on Washington's relationships with its allies. U.S. success in meeting the various challenges of the Middle East since 1945 has been mixed. Short-term success in Iran in 1954 was countered by the 1978 Islamic Revolution. Resolving the Arab-Israeli problem has complicated efforts to stabilize Middle Eastern oil production and even led to dangerous periods of shortages and price hikes. Although the Middle East may have been denied to the Soviet Union during the Cold War, important regional states – Libya, Iran, Iraq, Afghanistan – have to varying degrees been isolated from or even hostile to the Western world and its interests. Perhaps most distressingly, U.S. involvement in the Middle East has often precipitated major rows with the nation's key European allies. Such is certainly the case with the current war in Iraq, the Bush administration's trumpeted Coalition of the Willing notwithstanding. Without question, the deleterious effects of U.S. Middle Eastern policy on the nation's other foreign relationships has been one of the most far-reaching, if generally under appreciated, aspects of post-1945 U.S. foreign policy in the Middle East, and one that certainly deserves further scholarly attention.

---

58 «The National Security Strategy of the United States of America,» 17 September 2002, http://www.whitehouse.gov/nsc/nss.pdf (accessed 21 March 2005).

Index

Abadan, 78
Absolutism, 4, 9, 13, 16
Abu Ghraib prison, 47, 54
Acheson, 63, 64, 65, 66, 68, 69
Advisory Group on Public Democracy in the Arab and Muslim World, 48, 49
Afghanistan, XI, 3, 4, 8, 9, 11, 13, 14, 15, 16, 17, 18, 19, 40, 45, 46, 91, 92, 95
Africa, 4, 6, 17, 51, 77
Aguinaldo, Emilio, 38
Ajami, Fouad, 53
Al-Arabiyya, 49
Aleppo, 8
Alexander the Great, 4
Algeria, 33, 50, 88
Ali, Mehemet, 7, 8, 19
Allawi, Ayad, 48
Allen, David, 27
Allison, Robert, 41
al-Mani, Saleh A., 35
al-Mulk, Shah Shuja, 15, 16
al-Qaeda network, 41, 45, 53
America, *see* United States of America
American, X, XI, XII, 1, 3, 4, 7, 9, 16, 17, 24, 25, 26, 30, 31, 32, 34, 35, 36, 37, 38, 39, 40, 41, 42, 43, 46, 47, 48, 49, 50, 52, 53, 54, 56, 57, 62, 64, 65, 66, 67, 70, 74, 75, 80, 81, 85, 89, 92, 93; occupation of Iraq, X, 52; orientalism, XI, 39, 40; empire, 3, 20, 39, 41; radical right, 6, 12; foreign policy, 29, 56; policy in the Mediterreanean and Middle East, 30, 32, 43; cultural imperialism, 37; way of life, 50; imperialism, 50, 56; Zionist Committee, 70
American-Arab relationships, 35
Americans, XI, XII, 4, 7, 9, 17, 20, 31, 37, 38, 39, 40, 41, 44, 45, 46, 47, 48, 51, 52, 53, 54, 56, 58, 61, 70, 71, 73, 78, 82, 87, 88, 89, 92
Amirs of Sind, *see* Sind

Anglo-American, X, 9, 78, 83; Middle East, XI; Commission of Inquiry, 58; cooperation, 80, 81; alliance, 85
Anglo-French invasion of the Canal Zone, 11
Anglo-Iranian: oil company (AIOC), 30, 35, 77, 78, 79, 80; oil dispute, 77; settlement, 80
Anglo-Ottoman treaty of Balta Liman, 7
Anglo-Persian Oil Company, 77
Annexation, 7
Anti-Americanism, 19, 36
Anti-colonial, X
Anti-communism, 77
Anti-European-integrationism, 36
Anti-Semites, 59
Appeasement, 1, 45
Arab, X, XII, 30, 32, 33, 35, 36, 39, 41, 46, 47, 48, 49, 50, 51, 53, 54, 58, 60, 61, 66, 71, 72, 73, 74, 75, 83, 86, 87, 88, 89, 90; nationalism, X, 12, 53, 73; states, 6, 30, 32, 57, 59, 60, 61, 62, 64, 66, 67, 68, 70, 71, 72, 73, 74, 85, 86, 88, 90; world, 29, 30, 34, 35, 44, 49, 50, 51, 58, 69, 72, 74, 82, 86, 90; oil exporters, 34, 90; oil embargo, 35, 84, 86; radicals, 45, 52; Palestinians, 58; oil, 87, 88, 89
Arab-American groups, 46
Arab-European, XI
Arabia, 19
Arabian Gulf, 5
Arab-Israeli, 62, 68, 73, 74, 91, 94, 95; war, 59, 65, 90; conflict, 29, 69, 85, 88; settlement, 89, 90
Arabs, X, XI, 4, 29, 30, 32, 39, 40, 41, 45, 47, 48, 53, 54, 55, 73, 74, 85, 86, 87, 88, 89
Arafat, Yassir, 42, 43, 45, 56
Argentina, 19
Army of Retribution, 16
Ashanti, 8
Asia, X, 4, 5, 6, 8, 13, 14, 15, 16, 20, 38, 45, 51, 77, 92
Asiatic abolutism, 4
Aswan Dam, 82
Ataturk, Kemal, 48
Atlantic Motnhly, 43, 48
Atlantic, 37; Alliance, XII, 20, 88, 89; allies, 78
Attlee, Clement, 5, 58
Auckland, Lord, 4, 16
Australia, 19, 20
Austria, 17, 33

Index

Austrian Empire, 2
Axis of Evil, 41, 52

Baghdad, 5, 42, 46, 47, 49, 50, 52, 56, 94; Pact, 71, 81, 82
Bahrain, 18
Bain, Kenneth Ray, 58
Balance of power, XII, 80, 84
Balkans, 44
Baltimore, 46
Barbary Wars, 41
Barkley, Alben, 64
Barnett, Thomas, 51
Basra, X
Beijing, 14
Beirut, 49, 64, 73, 92
Belarus, 3
Belgium, 87, 93
Ben-Gurion, David, 63, 64, 65, 66, 67, 68, 70, 71, 72, 73, 74, 75
Bentham, Jeremy, 3, 9
Bentinck, Lord William, 4, 13
Bergus, Donald C., 74
Berlin, 29, 92; Wall, 11
Bernadotte, Count Folke, 59, 60, 61; plan, 60
Bey, Arabi, 8, 9
Bilateral, 62, 68, 69, 74, 81, 87
Bin Laden, Osama, 12, 41, 42, 45, 46, 47, 52, 54, 94
Black Sea, 8, 13, 14, 19
Blair, Tony, X, 20
Bloom, Sol, 63
Bosnian crisis, 18
Boykin, Jerry, 46, 47
Brandt, Willy, 26
Bremer, L. Paul, 52
Britain, X, XI, 1, 2, 3, 4, 5, 6, 7, 8, 9, 10, 11, 12, 13, 14, 16, 17, 18, 19, 20, 23, 24, 25, 26, 28, 29, 30, 31, 32, 33, 34, 40, 58, 63, 78, 79, 82, 83, 84, 85, 87, 89, 93
British, X, XI, 3, 4, 5, 7, 8, 9, 10, 12, 13, 14, 15, 16, 20, 25, 27, 28, 29, 32, 34, 35, 77, 78, 79, 80, 81, 82, 83, 84, 85, 87, 88; government, X, 24; forces, 6, 11; India, 10, 14; foreign policy, 20; ministers and diplomats, 24; influence in the Middle East, 40; Admiralty, 78; Foreign Office, 81, 83; officials, 82, 83; imperialism, 84

Britons, 4, 7, 9
Brown, Carl L., 4
Bukhara, 13, 14, 15, 16
Bureau of Near Eastern, South Asian, and African Affairs (NEA), 64, 65, 71, 72, 74
Burma, 19
Bush: George W., XI, 15, 37, 41, 42, 43, 45, 48, 49, 50, 51, 52, 53, 94; administration, 1, 3, 4, 6, 7, 8, 10, 11, 12, 13, 14, 15, 17, 18, 19, 20, 41, 42, 45, 47, 50, 51, 52, 53, 56, 95; George H. W. -, 10, 43, 48, 94
Baathist regime, 10

Caesar, 4
Cain, P.J., 2
Cairo, 5, 49, 56, 84
California, 46
Camp David Accords, 90
Canada, 17, 20, 33, 34
Capetown, 5
Caribbean, 25, 38
Carter, Jimmy, 18, 90, 92; Doctrine, 92; administration, 92
Castlereagh, Viscount, 11
Cellar, Emmanuel, 63
Central Asia, 5, 6, 8, 13, 14, 15, 16, 45, 51
Central Intelligence Agency (CIA), 50, 61, 64
Chalabi, Ahmad, 48
Chamberlain, Neville, 2
Cheney, Dick, 42, 48, 51
Chicago, 59
China, 12, 19; market, 38
Christendom, 14, 44
Christian, 42, 45, 46, 57, 62, 64, 92
Churchill, Winston S., 80
Clark University, 52
Clash of civilizations, 43, 44
Cleopatra, 4
Clifford, Clark, 68
Clinton, William Jefferson (Bill), 44, 94; administration, 43, 44, 45, 94
Coalition of the willing, XI, 95
Coalition Provisional Authority, 47, 48, 52
Cold war, X, 1, 3, 6, 9, 12, 16, 19, 20, 40, 43, 44, 45, 57, 74, 77, 79, 81, 84, 88, 94, 95

Collins, Billy, 54
Colonial, 3, 5, 7
Colorado, 47
Columbia University, 47
Comay, Michael, 62
Commission, *see* European
Common European foreign policy, 23, 24, 28, 31, 32, 35, 36
Common Foreign and Security Policy (CFSP), 23, 26
Communism, 40, 44, 52, 84
Communist, 78; Tudeh Party, 81; expansion, 85
Community, *see* European Economic Community
Concert of Europe, 9, 17
Conference of Presidents of Major American Jewish Organizations, 70
Conservative Political Action Conference (CPAC), 54
Containment, XI, 6, 40, 41, 43, 44, 45, 51, 71, 73, 84
Convention of London, 19
Copenhagen, 87; Report/Declaration, 23, 27, 29, 33
Coulter, Ann, 54
Council on American-Islamic Relations (CAIR), 53, 54
Council on Foreign Relations, 51
Crimea, 13
Crimean War, 13, 16
Crusade, 41, 43, 44, 45, 46
Cultural imperialism, XI, 38
Culture war, 16, 20
Czechoslovakia, 81

Dakar, 49, 83
Damascus, 49, 64
Davignon, Etienne, 31
De Atkine, Colonel Norvell, 47
de Gaulle, Charles, 24, 26, 31, 85
de la Serre, Françoise, 28
Defarges, Philippe Moreau, 28
Defense Department, XII, 64, 65, 69
Delhi, 5
Democrat, 42, 58, 60
Democratic peace theory, 17
Denmark, 23, 24

Dervishes, 8
Dewey, Thomas, 60
Dickinson College, 50
Diego Garcia, *see* Indian Ocean
Dien Bien Phu, 85
Dimona, 72
Djerejian, Edward, 48, 49, 50
Doctrine of containment, XI
Doctrine of preventive war, 51
Douglas-Home, Sir Alec, 29, 30, 32, 34
Dulles, 70, 73

Earl Grey administration, 6
East India Company, 4
Eastern Question, 4, 5, 20
Eban, Abba, 61, 64, 70, 72
Eden, Sir Anthony, 2
EEC, *see* European
Egypt, X, 3, 5, 7, 8, 9, 19, 20, 32, 33, 40, 47, 56, 61, 62, 70, 71, 79, 81, 82, 83, 84, 85, 86, 88, 90
Egyptian-Israeli peace treaty, 90
Eisenhower, XII, 70, 71, 72, 73, 82, 83; Dwight D. -, 2, 69, 81; administration, 6, 11, 69, 74, 81, 82; Doctrine, 71, 85
Elath, Eliahu, 63, 66, 68
Eliav, 74
Ellenborough, Lord, 14
Embargo, *see* Oil embargo
Empire, 1, 2, 3, 5, 9, 11, 14, 17, 18, 19, 20, 24, 25, 37, 38, 50, 52
England, *see* Britain
Entente Cordiale, 28
Epstein, Eliahu, 62
Equal suffering policy, 87
Esquire, 51
Ethridge, Mark, 65
EU, *see* European
Euphrates, 52
Eurasia, 4, 20
Europe, 5, 11, 12, 17, 24, 27, 30, 31, 34, 35, 36, 45, 58, 77, 88, 89

European, 4, 13, 14, 16, 20, 24, 36, 38, 83, 87, 88, 89, 90, 91, 93: Common Market, XI, 24, 25, 27, 29, 31, 34; states, 5, 17, 18, 35; Union (EU), XI, 17, 19, 24, 25, 27, 29; Economic Community (EEC/EC/Community), 23, 24, 25, 26, 27, 28, 29, 31, 32, 33, 34, 35, 36; Political Cooperation (EPC), 23, 26, 27, 31; Commission, 23, 25, 26, 27; Economic and Monetary Union (EMU), 23, 29, 34; Council, 23; integration, 26, 34, 35; policy on the Middle East, 27; Security and Cooperation, 28; Security Conference, 31; allies, 39, 90, 91, 95; Jewry, 57

Exxon, 39

Eyton, Walter, 65

Faisal, King, 86

Fashoda crisis, 18

Federal Communications Commission, 53

Ferguson, Neill, 8

First Afghan War, 8, 13

First Gulf War, *see* Gulf War

First World War (WW1), 4, 5, 9, 18, 77

Florida, 18, 46

Foreign Affairs, 44

Foreign and Commonwealth Office, 31

Foreign Ministry, 64, 66, 73

Fort Bragg, 47

Fort Carson, 47

Fox television network, 53, 54

France, 2, 17, 18, 19, 24, 25, 26, 28, 31, 33, 34, 63, 82, 83, 85, 87, 88, 89, 92, 93

Franco-British agreement, 24

Franco-Russian alliance, 11

Franks, Oliver, 62

Free trade, 7, 9, 12

French, 7, 25, 28, 31, 34, 40, 83, 85, 87, 88; government, 24, 26, 34; empire, 24-25; opposition to British EC membership, 29

Frum, David, 52, 53

Fundamentalism, 44, 93

Galilee, 65, 66

Gallagher, John, 4

Gaullist Party, 24

Gaza, 40, 43, 70, 71, 73

General Assembly, 59

German Federal Republic (BRD), 28, 33, 34
German: Empire, 2, 18; states, 28
Germany, 11, 17, 18, 19, 28, 32, 51, 60
Gladstone, William, 9, 20
Global power, 11, 37
Global war on terror, 41, 45, 46
Globalization, 1, 6, 9, 44; Functioning Core, 52
Golan Heights, 29, 40, 85, 86
Gorbachev era, 94
Grant, 37
Granville, Earl, 20
Great Britain, *see* Britain
Great Game in Asia, 4, 5, 6, 20
Great powers, 5, 11
Greece, 6, 20, 63, 79
Green threat, 43, 44, 45
Green, Theodore, F., 64
Greenhill, Sir Denis, 28, 31
Greenwich Village, 56
Gromyko, Andrei, 29
Ground Zero, 54, 56
Guantanamo Bay, 54
Gulf: War, 43, 53, 94; region, 93

Hague Summit, 26, 31
Hahn, Peter, L., XI, 39, 57, 84
Halliburton, 42
Hanoi, 55, 56
Hard power, XI
Harman, Abraham, 64
Harriman, W. Averell, 63
Hashemites, 10
Heath, Edward, 24, 25, 26, 29, 88
Hegemon, 1, 3, 10, 11, 17, 18, 19, 20, 95
Heiss, Mary Ann, XII, 77
Herat, 14, 19
Herlitz, Esther, 63, 64
Hersh, Seymour, 47, 48
Herzog, Yaacov, 71, 73

Hi, 49
Hijaz railway, 4
Hill, Christopher, 28
Hilldring, General John, 67
Hindu Kush, 16
Hindu superstition, 4
Hitler, Adolf, 2, 20
Holocaust, 57
Holy Alliance, 9, 11
Hopkins, 2
Hormuz, 11
House Foreign Affairs Committee (HFAC), 63
House Judiciary Committee, 63
Huleh controversy, 64
Hungary, 11, 83
Huntington, Samuel P., 44, 45
Hussein, Saddam, 9, 10, 11, 12, 14, 19, 41, 42, 43, 46, 48, 49, 51, 53, 94, 95
Hyderabad, 2
Haass, Richard. 50

Imperial, 5
Imperialism, 7, 38, 40
India, 3, 4, 5, 7, 10, 13, 14, 15, 16, 17, 19, 20, 78
Indian: Empire, 2, 5, 8, 13, 20; states system, 3, 14; Mutiny, 16; Ocean, 18
Indians, 14, 38
Indonesia, 19
Indus, 8, 15
Ingram, Edward, XI, 1
International Energy Agency, 89
Iran, 2, 3, 6, 10, 13, 15, 19, 30, 33, 40, 50, 56, 77, 78, 79, 80, 81, 82, 84, 91, 92, 94, 95
Iranian, 35, 78, 79, 80, 81, 84, 91, 93; nationalism, 78, 84; oil, 77, 78, 79, 80, 81; crisis, 80, 82, 83; Revolution, 81, 91
Iran-Iraq War, 93
Iraq, X, XI, 3, 8, 9, 10, 11, 12, 15, 17, 18, 19, 33, 37, 39, 41, 42, 43, 46, 47, 48, 49, 50, 51, 52, 53, 56, 93, 94, 95
Iraqi, 43, 46, 47, 49; army, 10, 52; invasion, 94
Ireland, 23, 24
Isandalwhana, 16
Islam, 4, 12, 19, 41, 43, 44, 45, 46, 48, 50, 52

Islamic, XI, 47, 48, 52, 53, 54; republic, 6, 10; dough; 12, 15; empires, 14; hatred of America, 39; radicals, 40, 41, 45, 46, 50; extremism, 43; fundamentalism, 44, 93; Revolution in Iran, 91, 95

Israel, X, 6, 29, 30, 32, 35, 39, 40, 41, 42, 43, 57, 59, 60, 61, 62, 63, 64, 65, 66, 67, 68, 69, 70, 71, 72, 73, 74, 75, 82, 85, 86, 87, 88, 90, 92; Defence Forces (IDF), 61, 62

Israeli, XI, 5, 6, 12, 29, 35, 40, 42, 53, 57, 60, 61, 62, 63, 64, 66, 67, 68, 70, 71, 72, 75, 82, 86; withdrawal from the occupied territories, 30, 33, 87; settlers, 30, 43; independence, 59; officials, 57, 60, 61, 62, 63, 64, 65, 67, 68, 69, 71, 72, 73, 74, 75; Foreign Ministry's United States Division (USD), 65

Israeli-American special relationship, 39, 42

Israeli-Palestinian: conflict, 42; peace agreement, 44

Italy, 17, 63, 92, 93

Jacobson, Eddie, 63, 66
Jaffa, 65, 66
Jalalabad, 16
Japan, 20, 51, 87, 89
Jarring, Gunnar, 29, 30, 31, 32
Javits, Jakob K., 63
Jeffersonian democracy, 50
Jerusalem, 33, 42, 56, 61, 64, 67, 68, 69, 85, 86
Jewish, XI, 42, 57, 58, 60, 61, 62, 63, 64, 66, 67, 70; settlement on the West Bank, 43; state, XI, 39, 57, 59, 75
Jews, 59, 60, 61, 62, 70
Jobert, Michel, 25
John F. Kennedy Special Warfare School, 47
Johns Hopkins University, 53
Jordan, 47, 49, 59, 62, 68, 73, 85; and Israel, 67
Jordanian crisis, 86
June War, 85

Kabul, 14, 15, 16, 46
Kandahar, 16
Kazakhstan, 6
Kenen, I.L., 70
Kennan, George, 45
Keren, Moshe, 65
Khan, Dost Muhammad, *see* Kabul
Khartoum, 5

Khiva, 13, 14
Khomeini, Ayatollah, 40
Kipling, Rudyard, 4
Kissinger, Henry, 29, 32, 33, 88, 89
Knox, Charles F. Jr., 61
Korea, 64, 79
Korean War, 6, 12
Kozyrev, S.P., 28, 31, 32
Kremlin, 40
Kut, 16
Kuwait, 3, 10, 12, 18, 33, 39, 43, 93, 94

Lake, Anthony, 44
Las Vegas, 54
Lausanne, 65, 66
Lawrence of Arabia, 4
Lawson, Edward B., 74
Lebanese civil war, 85
Lebanon, 47, 73, 92, 93
Lebanon-Jordan crisis, 70
Levant Company, 4
Lewis, Bernard, 43, 44, 45, 48, 49, 50
Liberal capitalism, 1, 7, 17
Libya, 33, 39, 88, 92, 93, 95
Lindh, John Walker, 46
Little, Douglas, XI, 37, 94
Lomé Conventions, 25
London, 30, 32, 78, 79, 81, 82, 83, 84
Lovett, Robert, 61, 62
Low Countries, *see* Netherlands
Luxembourg Report, 23
Luzon, 38

MacArthur, General Douglas, 9
Macaulay, George, 14
Macmillan, Harold, 20, 83, 84
Mahmud II, Sultan, 7, 19
Marshall, George C., 59, 62, 63, 68
Mart, Michelle, 74

McCarren-Walter Act, 46
McCarthy era, 46
McDonald, James G., 62, 63, 64, 67, 68
McKinley, 37
Mecca, 55
Mediterranean, 8, 13, 18, 19, 29, 30, 37, 56, 79, 82; power, 13; Programme, 25
Meir, Golda, 74
Members of Congress, 62, 63, 64, 68, 70
Mesopotamia, 8
Metternich, Prince, 6, 11
Middle East, X, XI, XII, 1, 2, 3, 4, 5, 6, 7, 10, 11, 12, 13, 15, 17, 18, 19, 20, 23, 27, 29, 30, 31, 32, 34, 35, 37, 38, 39, 40, 41, 42, 44, 45, 47, 48, 50, 51, 52, 53, 56, 57, 65, 72, 73, 75, 77, 78, 79, 80, 81, 82, 83, 84, 85, 86, 87, 88, 89, 90, 91, 92, 93, 94, 95; Peace Initiative, 48, 50; Defence Organization, 71, 82; Command, 82
Middle Eastern Studies, 43
Mill, James, 3
Milward, Alan, S., XI, 23
Mindanao, 38
Minh, Ho Chi, 56
Mogadishu, 47
Moroccan crisis, 18
Mosaddeq, Mohammad, 79, 80, 81; National Front, 78
Moscow, X, 14, 31, 40, 43, 61, 82, 83, 84, 91, 93
Mossadegh, Mohammed, 40,
Mosul, 8
Mother Jones, 42
Multilateral, 1, 17, 34, 49, 74
Munich, 23
Muslim, XI, 4, 21, 40, 43, 44, 45, 46, 48, 49, 51, 53, 54, 92; world, 37, 39, 41, 48, 49, 50, 51, 53, 54, 55; Americans, 46
Maastricht Treaty, 23

Napoleon III, 13
Napoleonic Empire, 17
Napoleonic Wars, 4, 11
Nasser, Gamal Abdel, 40, 56, 71, 72, 74, 81, 82, 83, 84
National Geographic, 41
National Guard, 8
National Security Council (NSC), 65, 73

National Security Strategy of the United States of America (NSS), 95
Nationalism, 60, 77, 84, 85, 90, 91
Nationalization, 77, 78, 79, 80, 81
Nawab of Bahawalpur, 15
Negev, 66
Nepal, 19
Netherlands, 17, 24, 34, 35, 84, 87, 88, 93
New York City, 37, 42, 50, 52, 54, 55, 56, 58, 64
New York Times, 46
Niles, David, 63, 69
Nixon, Richard M., 89
North Africa, 17, 51
North Atlantic Treaty Organization (NATO), 12, 82, 83, 85, 87, 88, 89, 90, 91, 93, 94
North Carolina, 47
North Yemen, X
Northern Tier, 6, 10
Norway, 24
Number Forty-One, *see* George H. W. Bush
Number Forty-Three, *see* George W. Bush

Ochakov crisis, 13
October War, 88
Oder-Neisse line, 28
Office of Homeland Security, 46
Oil, XII, 6, 12, 30, 32, 34, 35, 39, 40, 42, 43, 61, 77, 78, 80, 81, 82, 85, 86, 87, 88, 89, 90, 91, 92, 93, 94, 95; crisis, XI, 87; embargo, XI, 29, 33, 34, 86, 87, 88, 89, 90;
Olin Foundation, 44
Omdurman, 8
Operation Desert Shield, 10, 94
Operation Desert Storm, 10, 94
Operation Iraqi Freedom, 47, 48
Opium War, 19
Organization of Petroleum Exporting Countries (OPEC), 39, 42
Orientalism, 37, 40, 41, 45, 52
Orontes, 8
Ottoman: Empire, 5, 7, 8, 13, 17, 19; army, 14; Balkans, 17

Pacific, 25, 38
Pahlavi regime, 6

Pakistan, 6, 20, 92
Palestine, 30, 33, 55, 56, 57, 58, 59, 60, 78
Palestinian, 60, 69, 90, 92; suicide bombers, 42; terror, 42
Palestinians, 3, 5, 6, 12, 33, 49, 58, 59, 66, 92
Palmerston, Viscount, 3,4, 13, 19
Pan-Arab nationalism, 5, 82
Paris, 26; summit meating, 23
Patai, Raphael, 47, 48
Peace Corps, 8
Peace of Paris, 13
Pentagon, 39, 46, 47, 50, 57, 58
Perle, Richard, 52, 53
Persia, 4
Persian Connection, 10
Persian Gulf, X, 19, 39, 40, 51, 79, 91, 92, 93, 94
Peshawar, 8, 14
Petroleum, 34, 39, 42, 57, 77, 79, 90, 93
Philipines, 4, 38
Philippine Islands, 83
Pipes, Daniel, 45, 46
Poland, 17, 28
Pompidou, Georges, 24, 25, 26, 32, 34, 88
Porter, William J., 65
Portugal, 19, 88
Powell doctrine, 2, 19
Powell, Colin, 2, 48, 50
Project for a New American Century, 51, 56
Protocol of Troppau, 11
Punjab, 14, 16, 19

Qaddafi, Muammar, 92, 92
Qajar regime, 10, 11
Qatar, 33, 49
Qibya, 70

Rabat, 49
Racial hierarchy, XI
Rangoon, 5
Reagan, Ronald, 43; administration, 92

Red Army, 40
Red River territory, 8
Red Sea, 40
Red threat, 43, 44, 45
Reid, Ogden, 74,
Republican, 42, 58, 60
Rhode Island, 64
Ribicoff, Abraham A., 63
Rice, Condoleeza, 3, 21, 50, 51
Rissekappen, Thomas, 28
Road map to peace, 43
Robinson, Ronald, 4
Rogers, William, 32
Rome, 20
Roosevelt, Teddy, 37, 38; administration, 38
Rountree, William M., 72, 74
Rumsfeld, Donald, 9, 19, 42, 46, 51
Russia, XI, 6, 8, 12, 13, 14, 15, 17, 19
Russian, 7, 14, 19, 32; Empire, 4; expansion, 13

Sadat, Anwar, 86
Said, Ali Ahmed, 55
Said, Edward, 40
Saud, King, 74
Saudi Arabia, 10, 18, 33, 39, 42, 49, 80, 83, 86, 88, 90, 93, 94
Saudi regime, 12
Schlesinger, Dr. Laura, 46
Schlieffen Plan, 20
Second World War (WW2), 5, 6, 10, 18, 20, 28, 39, 77, 95
Security Treaty, 30
September 11, 2001, (9/11), 2, 41, 42, 45, 46, 47, 48, 50, 51, 54, 94
Serbian nationalists, 44
Shah, Mohammad Reza, 81, 91
Shaloub, Tony, 49
Sharansky, Natan, 53
Sharett, Moshe, 61, 62, 63, 67, 71
Sharon, Ariel, 43
Sikh confederacy, 14, 15, 19
Sinai, 29, 71, 73, 85, 86

Sind, 15, 16
Sindians, 15
Singapore, 5
Sisiphus, 4
Six Day War, X, 29, 30, 40, 85, 86
Soft power, XI
Somalia, 46
South Yemen, X
Soviet, 11, 29, 32, 39, 43, 53, 71, 72, 73, 77, 78, 79, 81, 83, 84, 85, 86, 88, 89, 91, 92, 93; Union (USSR), X, 6, 9, 10, 11, 12, 17, 28, 29, 30, 31, 32, 33, 40, 43, 45, 57, 79, 83, 84, 85, 88, 94, 95; influence, X, 90, 93; Communism, 6; invasion of Afghanistan, 11, 91; Russia, 36, 40; expansion, 73, 94; bloc, 72, 81, 82
Soviet-American tensions, 29
Soviet-Egyptian arms deal, 72
Spain, 38, 93
Special relationship, 20, 39, 42, 75
State Department, XII, 27, 40, 48, 49, 50, 57, 58, 60, 61, 62, 64, 65, 66, 67, 68, 69, 70, 71, 72, 84
State of the Union address, 51
Stevenson, Adlai, 70
Stewart, Michael, 31, 32
Sudan, X, 8
Suez, X, 78, 81, 82, 83, 84, 88; crisis, X, 1, 2, 82, 84, 85; Canal, 5, 6, 31, 78, 81, 82, 83
Suez-Sinai War, 70, 72
Superpower, 44, 51, 85, 86, 88
Supplemental Oil Agreement, 78
Sydney, 5
Syria, X, 3, 7, 8, 19, 50, 56, 83, 85, 88, 92

Tabriz, 7, 14
Taliban, 9, 18, 19, 40, 45, 46
Tehran, 80, 91
Tel Aviv, 39, 42, 61, 62, 63, 64, 67, 74, 85
Tel el-Kebir, 8
Terrorism, 12, 18, 19, 43, 45, 52, 92, 93
Thatcher, Margaret, 26
The Nation, 53
Third world war, 6, 10, 88
Tigris, 8, 55

Time, 54
Trabzon, 7, 14
Transcaucasia, 8
Treaty of Tilsit, 11
Trevelyan, Charles, 13, 14
Truman, Harry, XII, 20, 39, 43, 57, 58, 59, 60, 61, 62, 63, 64, 65, 66, 67, 68, 69, 70, 80; administration, XII, 6, 57, 59, 62, 80
Truman, Martha, 63
Turkey, 6, 18, 48, 79, 88
Twain, Mark, 37

Ukraine, 13
Unilateral, XII, 1, 11, 17, 19, 92, 93, 95
Unipolar, 3, 11, 16, 17
United Arab Republic (UAR), 71, 72
United Kingdom (UK), *see* Britain
United Nations, 9, 10, 11, 30, 32, 58, 59, 60, 61, 64, 67, 68, 72, 83, 94; Security Council, 30, 68; Resolution NO. 242, 30, 35, 87; Special Committee on Palestine (UNSCOP), 59
United States of America (US/USA), X, XI, XII, 1, 2, 3, 4, 6, 7, 8, 9, 10, 11, 12, 16, 17, 18, 19, 20, 27, 28, 29, 30, 32, 33, 34, 36, 37, 38, 39, 40, 41, 42, 43, 45, 46, 47, 48, 49 50, 51, 52, 53, 54, 56, 57, 59, 60, 61, 62, 63, 64, 65, 66, 67, 68, 69, 70, 71, 72, 73, 74, 75, 77, 78, 79, 80, 81, 82, 83, 84, 85, 86, 87, 88, 89, 90, 91, 92, 93, 94, 95; invasion of Iraq, 3, 11, 12, 15, 17, 42; Central Command (CENTCOM), 18, 92; multinationals, 39, 42; Army Special Forces, 46; Capitol, 53; officials, XI, 60, 67, 68, 70, 71, 72, 73, 74, 75, 77, 79, 80, 81, 82, 83, 84, 86, 88; government, 29, 41, 50, 60, 70, 75, 79, 80, 91; policymakers, 39, 40, 41, 43, 77, 79, 80, 81, 82, 90, 93, 94
US-Israeli relations, XI, 57, 60, 62, 70, 71, 73, 74, 75

Venezuela, 80
Venice Declaration, 90
Victoria, Queen, 3, 8
Vienna, 14; settlement, 17; system, 17, 18
Vietnam, 56, 92

Wall Street Journal, 53
Wall Street, 38
Warsaw Pact, 28
Washington Institute for Near East Policy, 44

Washington, 20, 25, 27, 29, 30, 32, 36, 38, 39, 40, 42, 43, 48, 49, 50, 52, 56, 62, 70, 71, 73, 77, 78, 80, 81, 82, 83, 84, 86, 88, 89, 90, 91, 92, 93, 94, 95; Energy Conference, 89
Webb, James E., 65, 66, 67
Weizmann, 66, 67
Wellesley, Marquis, 7
Wellington, Duke of, 8
West, 4, 6, 9, 10, 11, 12, 35, 36, 43, 44, 55, 57, 61, 79, 81, 83, 84, 85, 86, 88, 90, 91; Bank, 30, 40, 43, 85, 86; Point, 47; Germany, 87, 89
Western, XI, 1, 5, 6, 12, 33, 65, 69, 79, 80, 81, 82, 83, 84, 87, 89, 90, 91, 93, 95; power, X, 90, 94; technologies, XI, 8; European, XII, 31, 35, 82, 86, 87, 88, 89, 90; Europe, 17, 24, 26, 33, 34, 35, 79, 87, 93; world, 48, 95; interests, 40, 65, 71, 78, 80, 81, 82, 90, 91, 92, 93, 94; allies, 77, 85, 86, 93; control of Iranian oil, 78; alliance, 77, 79, 80, 85, 86, 89; domination of Iran's oil, 81; imperialism, 83, 84
White House, XII, 42, 48, 49, 53, 61, 62, 63, 64, 66, 68, 69, 75, 90
White Man's Burden, 4
White Paper of 1939, 58
William, Nassau Senior, 3
Wilson, Keith, 18
Wilson, Sir D., 31, 32
Wilsonian redemption, 53
Wolfowitz, Paul, 8, 45, 50, 51, 53
Wolseley, Sir Garnet, 8, 9
Woolsey, James, 44
World Trade Center, 55
Worldwide paramountcy, 3

Yaoundé Conventions, 24
Year of Europe, 29, 32, 89
Yergin, Daniel, 88
Yom Kippur, 58; War, 86, 87, 88, 89, 90
Yorktown, 16
Yugoslavia, 44, 51

Zahedi, Fazlollah, 81
Zionism, 57, 59, 69
Zionist: XII, 57, 58, 59, 60, 64, 70, 75